HOW TO SPONSOR PROJECTS

A PRACTICAL GUIDE TO SPONSORING PROJECTS AND BUSINESS CHANGE

CAROL DEVENEY

Copyright © 2023 by Carol Deveney

ISBN13: 9798392383528

All rights reserved.

No part of this book may be reproduced in any form or by any electronic or mechanical means, including information storage and retrieval systems, without written permission from the author, except for the use of brief quotations in a book review.

To sponsors.

CONTENTS

Introduction	9
1. WHAT IS A SPONSOR?	23
What does that mean?	23
What is the role of a Sponsor?	25
What do Sponsors need to know?	26
Who do Sponsor's report to?	28
Why should organisations have Sponsors?	33
Where do Sponsors work?	34
What background do you need to be a Sponsor?	35
Where should Sponsors be?	35
Reporting into Operations	36
Reporting to Project Managers	36
Matrix Organisations	37
Difference between Project Manager and Sponsor	38
Project Managers	38
Relationship between Sponsor and Project Management	39
Projects are hard work	40
The Unsuccessful Relationship	41
Top tips – What is Sponsorship?	44
2. STAKEHOLDER MANAGEMENT	45
What is Stakeholder Management?	45
Why Stakeholder Management Matters	46
Stakeholder Mapping	47
What Sponsors need to know about it	48
Types of Stakeholders	49
Campaign groups	49
Put yourself in the Stakeholder's shoes	51

    Resources to understand your External
    Stakeholders   52
    Public Sector   53
    Private Sector   55
    Trade Press   56
    Internal Stakeholders   56
    Industrial relations   56
    Managing Stakeholders when you don't love the project   58
    Stakeholder and bad news   60
    Top Tips for sharing bad news with stakeholders   61

3. MANAGING CHANGE   63
    What is managing change for Sponsors?   63
    Why it matters?   64
    Denial Phase   66
    Resistance Phase   67
    Exploration Phase   69
    Commitment Phase   71
    Planning changes that Alter Operations   72
    Top Tips for Managing Change   85

4. BENEFITS MANAGEMENT   88
    What is Benefits Management?   88
    Why Benefits Management Matters   88
    Benefits Mapping or Tracking   89
    What are the Benefits?   91
    Business change   93
    What Sponsors need to know about it   95
    Top Tips on Sponsor's Role in Benefits Management.   96

5. BUSINESS CASE   98
    What is a business case?   98
    Why do business cases matter?   100
    Sponsors own the Business Case   100

What do Sponsors need to know about it?	103
Stopping a project using a business case	103
When is enough, enough?	105
Cautionary tale	112
6. SCOPE	**117**
What is scope?	117
Scope	119
Requirements	119
Specifications	119
Client-driven scope change	122
7. GOVERNANCE	**126**
What is Governance?	126
Corporate Governance	126
Project Governance	127
Why does it matter?	127
Leading Governance	128
What not to do?	132
Stage gates	133
Change control	135
Top Tips for Successful Stage Gate Reviews	138
8. ASSURANCE	**139**
What is Assurance?	139
Why Assurance matters	140
What Sponsors need to know about it	141
Types of Assurance	141
Top Tips for Success Leading Assurance	144
9. FUNDING AND COMMERCIAL RISK	**146**
What are Funding and Commercial risks?	146
Why it matters?	147
Funding and finance	148
Private Sector	148
Funding	149
Leading Corporate Risk	150
Commercial acumen	155

Supply chains 155
Top Tips for Success 156

10. LEADERSHIP 158
What is Leadership? 158
Why it matters 159
How do you know if you are a Dream Sponsor? 161
How do you know if you are a Dreaded Sponsor? 163
What leadership qualities do you need to be a Sponsor? 164
What experience do you need to be a Sponsor? 165
Giving Strategic Direction as a Leader 165
Personal Effectiveness 166
The busy Sponsor 169
Playing the fiddle or conducting the orchestra 172
Doing versus making sure it is done 174
Resilience 175
Top Tips to Go from Busy to Productive 177
Tops tips on scheduling for Sponsors 179

11. PROJECT LIFECYCLE 181
Project lifecycle approaches 182

About the Author 187
Acknowledgments 191

INTRODUCTION

If you have started the journey of being a Sponsor you are getting used to explaining many times what being a Sponsor means. You've probably told people more times than you ever thought that you would. Perhaps you already wonder if there is anyone left who doesn't yet know.

It is easier to explain to people who work in a world of projects or change management but once you step out of that world the explanation becomes tougher and more complex. Trying to describe how you have a job managing ambiguity in a way that changes with every project is ambiguous in itself.

This book will teach you the basics of being a Sponsor. It will also give you a narrative to help explain to your colleagues, friends, and family what your job is.

Being a Sponsor is a crucial role in projects and change management. It is the role that has the most impact on the

INTRODUCTION

likelihood of success and whether the project will deliver the benefits or not.

The Sponsor is ultimately accountable for the success of a project, programme, or business change. They are the guiding mind of the project throughout and lead the project to make sure the business gets what it wants from the project.

Being a Sponsor, however, can feel vague and uncertain. Knowing how to change that can feel harder than just ploughing on and doing your best and hoping it is good enough.

Surely Sponsors and projects deserve better than muddling through. Not knowing what you are expected to achieve is not only challenging, it is demotivating. It makes a hard job harder.

Many Sponsors start searching for answers in their own companies. They ask 'What is the role of a Sponsor in this company?

They hear answers such as:

"If you figure it out tell us."

"If I tell you I'd have to kill you."

"Whatever you want it to be."

"Not project management."

"Getting the money and leaving the project people alone."

INTRODUCTION

"An extra job on top of your day job."

"All blame and no thanks."

All highly amusing, but also very worrying when no one around you knows what you are expected to do. An absence of agreement on how you should do it, what you should be doing, and what good or bad looks like exists in response to many Sponsors asking the question.

To understand the role, what it means, how to do it, and what good looks like, Sponsors have to start on a research trail of their own. Twisting and turning through associated materials, hand-me-down advice and the occasional opening of a magical vault with some pearls of wisdom inside.

It seems odd that the role of the Sponsor is the least well-understood of all the project professions. The work is important because benefits are the entire reason for spending time and money on projects in the first place.

It is also the least well-served with professional institutions, resources, research and publications. There is no seminal text that everyone turns to when they want to know how to be a Sponsor.

Many Sponsors figure it out as they go on their first project. They adapt and adjust and help carve out what it means to be a Sponsor. Then that project ends, and the next project has a different set of stakeholders, outcomes, and challenges. It looks like what they tried last time won't work this time. Yet their organisation is still unsure of the role of the Sponsor, so the Sponsor has to start reinventing their role or reapply what they tried last time.

The inability to replicate success becomes exhausting and burnout rates are high amongst the Sponsor community. It is the highest in organisations with low levels of maturity of the role of the Sponsor.

Even Sponsors who are experienced in the operations of their business environment and embrace change find it hard to ever achieve anything in environments where being a Sponsor lacks definition and maturity.

When you are uncertain about what your role as Sponsor is how can you be successful at doing it? How can you measure your success over time if you don't know what good looks like? Many people do have a view of what bad Sponsors look like! That isn't always that helpful though as it just creates a list of things not to do. That is hardly a recipe for successful and effective Sponsors.

The role of a Sponsor is one that helps projects be successful, enables people, and has a very clear role in managing the ambiguity in change management or projects. That is an exceptionally difficult role to execute without someone telling you what that looks like, how to do it, when to do it, and how to know if you are getting it right.

When Sponsors start in the role they can often feel like every new day or project stage brings a new set of surprises.

INTRODUCTION

Unplanned and unpredictable pitfalls around every corner lead to Sponsors feeling like they are all reactions and no strategy. Plate spinning is how many Sponsors describe their main planning activity.

So many of us Sponsors have this experience that it has become normalised. We grow accustomed to a diet of stress, high-octane adventures, and busyness.

What if there was a better way? What if the core components of the role of a Sponsor can be identified and described?

What if a series of steps could be laid out as a framework for successful Sponsorship that can be applied to every project and every business operation?

What if there is a way that a Sponsor can learn and apply to make their role repeatable with some easy adaptions for each project?

That is what this book is going to do for you. The secret to the success of being a great Sponsor is learning how to mature your competence over time and consistently getting better by planning what great looks like and working towards it.

Sponsorship is contextual and needs an element of bespoke tailoring in each environment that it is embedded into as a professional discipline or way of getting things done. There are many parts of the role of a Sponsor along with techniques, tools, solutions, and behaviours that if you adopt and

INTRODUCTION

apply consistently your job will become easier and more successful.

This book will share with you the most impactful of these and give you advice about how you can apply them in your situation or context.

As you work through each chapter you will notice straight away that you are more adept at some Sponsor areas than others. That is great news as you already maturing as a Sponsor and can plan which areas you want to develop next. Then you can apply the advice in that chapter. You can work through it in sequence, or you can choose the area that you think getting better at will give you the most benefits if you improve in that area.

After covering in detail what a Sponsor is and which organisations should have them the key areas of focus for a Sponsor are explained in depth. There are eleven subject areas. For each area, this book covers:

- What the subject is.
- Why it matters.
- What Sponsors need to know about it.
- Top tips for success.

The key areas to focus on are:

1. What is a Sponsor?
2. Stakeholder management.

INTRODUCTION

3. Managing change.
4. Benefits management.
5. Business case.
6. Scope.
7. Governance.
8. Assurance.
9. Funding and commercial risk.
10. Leadership.
11. Project Lifecycles.

There is an examination of how to be an effective Sponsor in each of the subject areas. There is brief guidance on applying an effective sponsor lifecycle to the variety of project lifecycles you may come across.

In writing this book, I have drawn on my almost twenty years as a Sponsor and my extensive discussion and research with a network of Sponsors who work in a variety of environments and project types.

I was a Sponsor before I knew it. I was called a Project Manager at the time that I was recruited to be a Sponsor. I was managing a small portfolio of projects and programmes but in reality, I was doing the work I came to later recognise as Sponsorship.

I was managing the stakeholders, collating and governing funding, setting and monitoring outcomes for others to deliver against whilst I assured the progress. All far closer to Sponsorship than project management.

INTRODUCTION

When I made the switch officially to being a Sponsor it was a big step change. I went from managing £1m in my portfolio to being part of a Sponsor team where 3 of us sponsored a £300m project reporting to a lead Sponsor.

My journey from there led to me being the lead Sponsor on a £360m project. It eventually led to me becoming Head of Sponsorship for that organisation with a reporting accountability for the assurance and benefits to the executive team and board of a portfolio of £42 billion.

Headhunted from there to take Sponsorship as a profession in Canada I loved adapting Sponsorship to a new context and continent. I went from there straight into starting a Sponsorship consultancy business called See Change International Consulting Ltd. See Change has trained hundreds of Sponsors across the world and worked with many large organisations to help them establish, embed or improve their Sponsorship capability.

Since then, the company has grown and so has my Sponsor network.

Sponsorship is a profession I love being part of. I have grown my Sponsor network consistently and it now reaches different countries and industries.

I don't have a degree in Sponsorship as that doesn't exist! My academic background is in business and leadership. Due to the nature of the types of projects I have sponsored, I have

INTRODUCTION

also become dual-qualified in Health and Safety and Environmental Management. Over time I have also added to my business qualifications with postgraduate and short-course learning at some of the top UK business schools.

These combined with technical progression in change management, project management, and infrastructure delivery have helped me collate a set of skills that have enabled me to work with some of the best teams in the world.

Of course, that means making a lot of mistakes along the way. The gift that keeps on giving is to look at those mistakes and use hindsight to turn them into lessons that I am open to sharing with others in the hope they can find something useful in creating a different course of action for their project.

I have been fortunate enough to have many people share their stories with me too and some of these form the basis of the advice in this book. Albeit some of it had to be anonymised to protect the innocent and sometimes the guilty!

You will have noticed too that the role of a Sponsor involves managing complexity and ambiguity. That is highly contextual. To give you the insights that you are looking for into how to understand and do the role this book will also expose the details that lie under the surface of the work that Sponsors do.

INTRODUCTION

The challenge of being a Sponsor may often be a technical one in terms of organisational development, learning, development, and competency.

The reality though is that all of that translates into a personal and sometimes painful experience.

When no one knows what it is and there is not much training. When the organisational understanding and maturity of it are low.

When there is so little structure that everything that happens in your project feels like a surprise. And worse, a surprise that you should somehow have anticipated and headed off but didn't.

Where there is nothing to describe what good looks like in a consistent format.

When people don't understand it or value what you do as a Sponsor.

Then whether you are a full-time Sponsor or have had 'Sponsor' added to your already enormous work pile it feels personal.

It makes a tough job tougher. it makes you feel like you are not always sure if you are doing it well.

You may compare yourself to others but if their context is even slightly different how do you know if you are doing it well or not compared to them?

INTRODUCTION

This side of what is a very exciting and rewarding job makes it exhausting. It can feel like success is an ever-elusive measure always slightly out of reach.

Whenever I say to a room full of Sponsors that it is a lonely role I see vociferous agreement. You are in a role where you are bridging the gap between two teams or sets of stakeholders. Not fully part of a project team and not fully part of the business team. At least not until you establish trust and people see that you are a valuable part of both. In the meantime, you are in a bridging role.

Even when you show your professionalism and move through the team getting to know, like, and trust you it can still be lonely. As the person accountable for project governance, you will also have to keep a certain independence from both teams. After all, you represent the benefits and that has to be your laser focus throughout.

That requires a great deal of resistance to being personally swayed into being a member of a particular camp.

So loneliness comes with independence and is something that you cannot remove. You can mitigate it. You do that by establishing trusted relationships with others who can support you. My own experience leads me to know that other Sponsors understand this challenge and how to navigate it better than anyone else you will encounter.

It is a nuance of being a Sponsor best supported by other Sponsors. Creating that network of supportive sponsors is

INTRODUCTION

something I encourage you do to now and to grow throughout your Sponsorship career.

I still call up the role models I had seventeen years ago and seek their advice or counsel on Sponsors' subjects. They will provide the emotional support and personal advice that you need to navigate the rough waters of being a Sponsor.

When you put down this book you will find it easier than before to do your job.

Rather than having to create a bespoke solution from scratch each time you are faced with a Sponsor problem, you will be able to start to see patterns and similarities. You will be able to plan for these.

Then you can start to apply these tools and approaches to make your life easier, your projects better and deliver your project benefits with more ease and confidence.

When Sponsors understand what their role is, how it is different from other project roles, and how to apply solutions in a reapable and maturing way they start to find the role easier. They settle into their confidence and make decisions more easily. They drive and lead projects instead of reacting to issues as they arise.

Their projects and project teams start to flourish too and delivery of benefits is not only easier but also more likely to happen. They hand back projects to clients, funders, and operational teams that are complete, that work, and that

INTRODUCTION

reduce the project and change fatigue so common in large organisations.

If you follow this step-by-step guide towards successful sponsorship then you will be able to plan out a route from overwhelmed, reactive Sponsor to effective, successful Sponsor.

Try not to worry about missing the stress and busyness too much. Projects will always have that adrenaline-fuelled pace. You will be able to reserve that for the exceptional instead of using it every day.

Let me begin by taking you through what the role of a Sponsor is and why organisations should have Sponsors. Then I will help you move forward with bringing sponsorship into your organisation or being a Sponsor.

1

WHAT IS A SPONSOR?

There are many definitions of a Sponsor used in companies and in professional institutions concerned with project or change management. These tend to use the terminology of their professions. Whilst these are valid and will be discussed later in this book it is time to start with a simple explanation.

The Sponsor leads a project to make sure the benefits are delivered.

What does that mean?

The Sponsor is the person accountable for identifying what a project is meant to achieve at the start and for making sure that is what happens by the end.

The Sponsor is ultimately accountable for the success of a project or business change. They are the guiding mind of the project throughout and lead it in line with the strategy to make sure the business gets what it wants from the project.

It can be a full-time role or it can also be a side role added to the day job of a senior person in an organisation.

The Sponsor is appointed by the company making the change to start a project and see it through to the end and bring about some desired change or benefits.

That does not of course mean that the whole weight of support of the company is thrown behind the Sponsor to help them succeed. Not everyone in a company wants a change to occur, even when it is beneficial or can be a matter of survival for the company itself.

The Sponsor can end up leading a project that many in the company do not want to see happen. The Sponsor can be working with a project team who sees the Sponsor as part of the company team rather than as part of the project team. In truth, the Sponsor is the bridge between the two and this can make it a lonely role for the Sponsor.

Being the bridge between the business operation and the project team bringing about the change can leave Sponsors feeling exposed, vulnerable, and having a lot asked of them. Sponsors occupy this challenging space and have to navigate it carefully and courageously if they are to have any chance of success.

The following chapters will look at some of the pitfalls and practical solutions that Sponsors can use to do that.

What is the role of a Sponsor?

The Sponsor is the person who is ultimately accountable for the delivery of the benefits of a project.

The Sponsor's role is focused on outcomes. They have to have a relentless focus on the benefits, the end state, the purpose, and the vision. They are more focused on whether or not the project will deliver a return on investment than the detail of how it will be done. Sometimes described as a balancing act, a cog in the machine, or the crank handle and they are all good analogies.

The role of the Sponsor is closely linked to the context in which they operate. The exact duties that Sponsors undertake will vary based on the type of project they are working on, the industry, and the commercial structure.

A Sponsor owns the business case and is accountable for the delivery of the benefits. They're also the central link between business as usual in the operating environment, stakeholders, and the project delivery team. The role of a Sponsor includes initiating and leading the project and acting on behalf of the client. Sponsors work with clients to agree on what benefits they want to achieve from the investment that they are making and help clients to translate their wants and needs into a set of requirements. Sponsors also give direction motivation and support throughout the project life cycle to the project team whilst keeping stakeholders informed and aligned and resolving any strategic challenges that the project faces.

What do Sponsors need to know?

What does it mean to be a Sponsor? The Oxford English dictionary describes the word Sponsor as a verb: "To arrange for something to take place". How does that translate into the noun when we look at someone whose professional role is as a Sponsor?

Although it is still struggling to gain the same recognition and understanding as many of the other project disciplines such as project management and programme controls, Sponsorship is now considered a profession by many people and companies.

Sponsorship is no dark art or mystery profession. It is like many of the project disciplines. It is a collection of tasks and activities that are grouped under the accountability of one job role.

The job description of a Sponsor varies from one organisation to the other. That is no different from any other profession, discipline, or job. What remains the same is the core elements that make the role that of a Sponsor.

There may be some variations, additions, or subtractions but there are some generally agreed accountabilities that most people would recognise as grouped together being the role of the Sponsor. These are:

- Benefits management and realisation.
- Owning the business case.
- Leading the strategic direction.
- Stakeholder management.
- Securing funding.
- Managing the scope.
- Governance and assurance.
- Change management.
- Owning the client relationship.
- Project advocacy.

Some organisations have other aspects that Sponsors control based on their structure and how they deliver projects. These can include:

- Control of contingency.
- Leading communications and marketing.
- Reporting to the board.
- Management of regulators.
- Political lobbying.
- Media and external briefings.

It is also common for Sponsors to have a role in either being accountable for or at least signing off at each stage of a gated project process. This forms a central part of the role of a Sponsor in project governance and yet it is often overlooked or seen as being solely the role of the project team with a report back to the Sponsor. We will look more at governance in Chapter 7.

Who do Sponsor's report to?

Who Sponsors report to does depend somewhat on the organisational structure. What I have seen to be common everywhere is that, unlike many jobs or roles, a Sponsor always has more than one reporting line. This is because they will have a line management structure that may align with a department, business unit, or team. Then they will also have a reporting line for the project. This could be into a more senior Sponsor in a multi-Sponsor team. It could also be into a steering group, board, executive committee, funder, client, or direct to a chief executive or chair.

What is certain is that Sponsors will find themselves reporting to more groups and levels the higher the profile and/or complexity of the project. This is where Sponsors can add value by providing a consistent source of truth and reporting that keeps the right people informed at the right time. This might stop some people from 'shopping around' for project updates and it is a way Sponsors can reduce that. This also helps the project team by having clear lines of communication and reporting of information established and knowing that they can refer those who like to shop for project titbits back to the Sponsor.

A layer of complexity can exist around who is the client for a project. This, at times, is the operational department that will receive the asset built or impact of business change and have to run that as a future operational part of the business. It can also be the board of the company that forms a group that acts as the client. It may also be that a steering group is established for the duration of the project and this group acts as a client.

At times the steering group will be established by the Sponsor who will chair it throughout the life of the project to oversee its success. In this case, the board or funder are often the clients. Funders are not always directly the client, especially in the case of public-sector-funded infrastructure projects. In those cases, the funder is likely to be the government itself with the funding allocated and administered by a particular government department. They will wish to be involved, informed, and make decisions. However, they are often not the eventual asset operators.

A simple structure of the board as a client who is also the funder works well. Sponsors rarely have such simplicity of arrangement on all projects. Therefore, understanding that picture from the outset is crucial.

Some key questions to ask are:

- Who will own the asset or business change impact beyond the project lifespan?
- Who will operate the asset or business change impact beyond the project lifespan?
- Who is funding the project?
- Who is funding the asset in the future?
- Who is the client?

Who is the client should be an easy question, yet over years of auditing and preview projects it has proved to be one that Sponsors have time and again wrestled with. In mature organisations ask a project manager who is your client and the answer is often without hesitation 'the Sponsor'. So why is it more difficult for Sponsors to answer when they are often the people who own the 'client' relationships?

There will be some Sponsors reading with a raised eyebrow at the prospect of not having clarity over the Client. They will be accustomed to a very clear line of sight to the client. It is of course the board or the chief executive or the business lead for the unit requesting the change or it is the funder. The good news for you is you can skip the next few paragraphs if you don't intend to move jobs.

In some organisations who the client is can be harder to pin down. There may be several individuals or groups with a belief that they are the client. It is likely there is a good reason for the individuals to think they are the client. It is important to seek to understand that, clarify it, and be honest about the range and reach that they will have in project decisions before proceeding. If not you risk a very disgruntled stakeholder and a lot of people with loud voices and no voting power derailing your project.

Once you know who they are clients enjoy:

- Assurance.
- No surprises.
- Regular, consistent reporting in a format that they can use.
- Good news to deliver up the chain of command.
- PR opportunities.
- Early warning of issues with insight as to when to take action and when to just be aware.
- Confirmation of when issues are resolved.
- Sponsors who take accountability when things go wrong.

An experienced client of a major portfolio who deals with multiple Sponsors at any one time said

"I pay the Sponsor to deliver us benefits. When it is going wrong, I don't want to hear from them how it is the project manager's fault and they did everything they could. If they can't prevent project failure, why am I paying for a Sponsor?

Maybe I should have just spent that money on a more experienced project manager or two project managers"

The best Sponsors will willingly stand back and let the client take the credit at the successful end of the project. If you want to be cutting ribbons and clutching accolades, then a career in sponsorship may not be for you.

The pain, tears, and anguish of getting projects over the finish line may make it feel like you should be the hero of the day. In reality, that honour belongs to your client. Your role was to implement their vision and invest their funding in outcomes. The credit for those outcomes rests with the client. In the public sector that often means elected officials cutting ribbons alongside local residents or user groups. In the private sector, it often means chief executives or celebrities alongside those user groups. Help deliver those successful outcomes and photo opportunities, and your reward will be the opportunity for you or your organisation to deliver more projects or receive future investments from those clients.

The Sponsor has a role play to in celebrating the success of the project. A good Sponsor will likely be involved in opening events along with the obligatory trade and professional awards. A great Sponsor understands the balance between being involved and giving your client the limelight.

As well as Sponsors understanding their role it is important that steering committees, boards, funders, and clients take time to understand the role of the Sponsors. Paying attention to how they enable the Sponsor to succeed is one of the activities that they can take to get better returns from investments in projects. If a steering committee executive or board struggles to describe accurately what they ask and expect from a Sponsor their chances of succeeding are inhibited.

Why should organisations have Sponsors?

In a large company having Sponsors can be beneficial. If a business never runs projects or undertakes business change, in short, they do not need Sponsors. Certainly, there are departments and business areas which often don't need sponsorship. These are departments that are completely operational and not in need of significant change. These departments are far better served by continuous improvement experts.

Large companies or departments with regular projects, a project portfolio, or regular significant business changes will also benefit from having Sponsors. This can mean employing people permanently who are professional Sponsors. It can also mean creating the competency and capability for Sponsorship with existing employees who are trained in sponsorship.

There is of course the option to just drop the Sponsorship of a project or change as an 'extra' on someone's desk. It is rarely successful or effective for the project and certainly not for the Sponsor!

The aim is to have Effective Sponsorship. Why? Well, we know that it makes a significant difference.

The Project Management Institute's 2015 'Pulse of the Profession Study' research tells us that when there are engaged Sponsors on more than 80% of projects

- 77% meet original goals (compared with 46%)
- 77% meet original goals (compared with 46%)
- 66% finish within the original budget (compared with 40%)
- 10% avoid outright failure (compared with 20%)

The comparison here is against projects without an engaged Sponsor.

This points to engaged Sponsors being critical to the success of companies meeting their project and change objectives. The Sponsor behaviours that help or hinder projects are described in Chapter 10.

Where do Sponsors work?

Sponsors work anywhere there is a change happening. Projects by their nature are about change. Whether that is changing people, places, or systems. You will find Sponsors leading change through projects in various industries including:

- Infrastructure projects such as housing, rail, air, and roads.
- Healthcare companies.
- Charity and Voluntary organisations.
- Property companies.
- IT and software.
- Banking.
- Oil and Gas.

What background do you need to be a Sponsor?

Sponsors come from a diverse range of academic and work experience backgrounds including:

- Business and leadership backgrounds.
- Change management.
- Engineering.
- Legal.
- Accounting.
- Communications.
- Sales.
- Operational backgrounds in their industry.
- Project management disciplines.

Where should Sponsors be?

The question of whether Sponsors should be part of a corporate function or whether they should be embedded in the business units of an organisation is wrestled with in many organisations. There is an infinite number of options. Below we explore some of the most common structures. Of importance here are organisational structure, authority, maturity of the organisation, mandate, and capability of Sponsors.

Reporting into Operations

This can work well as the owner of the business operation is often the receiver of the output and/or outcome of the project and perhaps also the benefits. The tension between operations and projects can be well managed by an experienced Sponsor whose home base is in operations. That said, it can be a challenge for the Sponsor to get adequate support if the operations team is faced with the tactical and daily challenges that the business demands they focus on.

Reporting to Project Managers

Sponsors cannot be effective when they report to the project manager as this loses credibility on governance and assurance. It also subsumes the authority of the role and creates an extra resource for the project manager. Observations of this in action have demonstrated that the Sponsor becomes a resource supplement based on their predominant skill set. They either become an additional commercial manager, a stakeholder manager, or on some occasions an informed technical and operations support.

Matrix Organisations

Some like having Sponsors who are flexible and move around to be in the right place. They can be embedded in business units as individual sponsors or skill sets of people in departments where it is needed. Of course, the size of the organisation matters. A small organisation is not going to maintain a standing supply of Sponsors in case of major business changes or projects occurring.

An organisation with frequent projects or whose main business is projects or change management would be wise to do so. What about some of the downtime? If you have racehorses you don't race them every day. You rest them between races. This rest time for Sponsors is the time that they use to build relationships with stakeholders, investigate the existing state, monitor benefits, and review lessons learned from previous projects.

It is more important to have the authority delegated from the relevant part of the organisation to be able to have some effective levers than to focus overly on the organisational structure. This is especially true in organisations that have 'reorganisation mania' or are on a steep curve of either growth or maturity.

The reality is that Sponsors can thrive anywhere when they are:

- In a part of the business that welcomes them.
- In a company that is clear about what accountability it delegates to Sponsors.
- In a company that is clear about what it expects from Sponsors.
- Offered training, competency, and capacity management.
- Given appropriate strategic structure with the freedom to tailor tactical for their projects
- Valued.

Difference between Project Manager and Sponsor

Project Managers

Many Sponsors end up with 'profession explanation fatigue'. They end up just agreeing when someone says, "So you are sort of a project manager then?". Some Sponsors continue to explain the role of the Sponsor until either the light bulb moment happens, or listener fatigue leads to a pretence of comprehension.

Some Sponsors, like the author, came to sponsorship from project management. Sponsors predominantly work on change since change to a business, an asset, or infrastructure is normally managed as a project then it can seem like a sensible shorthand to say that Sponsorship = Project Management.

However, that overlooks the fundamental differences in the roles and the different parts that they both play in successful projects. Both of these roles are important. The difference in accountabilities between the two and how to make that work successfully in practice is also covered in this chapter.

Project management accountabilities sit within the boundaries of time, cost, scope, and quality.

Sponsors' accountabilities sit within the boundaries of benefits, business cases, stakeholders, and requirements.

Relationship between Sponsor and Project Management

Like all strong relationships, that between a project manager and a Sponsor is best built on a strong foundation of trust. From the initiation of the idea that turns into a project and onto a finished outcome, your success is bound up with each other.

You may be able to succeed despite each other but be under no allusion that this will be difficult. It will endanger the benefits and put enormous strain on each side of your respective accountabilities, not to mention the personal toll on each of you.

It is far more productive to succeed because of each other.

The chances are that you have different predominant skill sets from each other, hence your differing roles. Perhaps you have different personality types. You most certainly have different roles. You do have a shared objective which is a successful outcome from the project that you are both working on. You need no better reason to unite and work together to achieve that outcome.

Projects are hard work

Whichever project management method or tool you are using will come with a set of recommended documents. Somewhere in there will be a document on role maps, organisation charts, or a RACI chart (Responsible, Accountable, Consulted, Informed) all useful tools.

Sponsors, set them aside for a few hours and invest that time in a quality discussion with your project management counterpart to talk about the detail of what you will each be doing.

- Avoid shying away from contentious areas.
- Get into the spaces where you worry you may cross over and talk about them to resolve them now.
- Clarify roles with each other and the business.
- Get clear on understanding key lines of communications and where you don't mind crossover.
- Share how you tend to react in a crisis.

- Talk about how you like to work, and what your preferred communication styles are.
- Discuss those really difficult stakeholders and be honest about which of you has the best rapport with them.
- As uncomfortable as it may be, share any skills or knowledge gaps with each other.

With any luck, you will be able to support each other in skills or knowledge gaps. With good planning, you will find or recruit others to the team who have the skills needed to counteract them or fill any gaps that you identify.

You are the management team of this project and the relationship that you have with each other will set the tone for the project environment. The integrity of your relationship will become a driving force for good during difficult times and at key decision stages. Dysfunctions in your relationships will permeate your team and those dysfunctions will become a risk in your project.

It will create the single biggest determining factor of success on a project: The successful relationship.

The Unsuccessful Relationship

When relationships aren't working, they have a detrimental impact on projects and teams no matter how much we may try to ignore or avoid them. Out of loyalty or fear your teams may not talk too openly about broken relationships in the leadership team.

If this happens in your project you have two choices:

1. Blame the project manager and watch your project struggle.
2. Take action to improve it.

If you choose option one you may want to rethink a career in sponsorship! If you buy into making the other person, the problem then be under no illusion that you are anything less than part of the problem. You are accountable for success on this project and the relationship with the project manager is at least 50% on you.

If others in the project or the business recognise and highlight issues between both of you this is emblematic of the problem spiralling. They will be frustrated if they are caught between both of you. This is sometimes the outcome of a dysfunctional project leadership team when the Client, Sponsor, and Project Manager all work for the same organisation.

It can also happen when the client is in an external organisation and both parties have regular contact with both of you or your teams. In either case, they will note the lack of clarity of purpose or failure to engage in a way that positively impacts the project and benefits. You don't have to be the best of pals. You do have to be professionals who work together effectively and impactfully.

If you are lucky clients may mention it or escalate the issue of these unsuccessful relationships, giving you the chance to resolve it. If you are unlucky or fail to seek regular client updates on how they view performance or relationships then you may never hear a word from them about it.

Not because they aren't speaking about it. They are just not speaking to you about it. But they are speaking about it. To their teams, their board, your other clients, their managers, to other client organisations, to their significant others. Perhaps even to your project manager and your team. In short to everyone who is willing to listen and who is not you. This is dangerous territory for a Sponsor. It is both detrimental to your project and risking your reputation, integrity, and project.

Informed clients rightly expect that the Sponsor will manage the stakeholders and relationships in a professional way and with the aplomb of a diplomatic ambassador. Therefore, troubles between you and the project manager are something that you are expected to have the skill set and willingness to resolve without them impacting the project or the client.

During peer reviews or audits, there is a certain sublanguage and set of phrases that auditors and assurers are tuned into that expose very quickly dysfunction between the project manager and Sponsor. There is little chance you will be able to hide it from them so it's worth taking the uncomfortable action of addressing and repairing the relationship.

Top tips – What is Sponsorship?

What it is

- A project profession.
- Contextual.
- A way of managing ambiguity.
- About benefits.

What it is not

- A business-as-usual activity.
- Clear, defined, and repeatable.
- A linear activity.
- About building things.

2

STAKEHOLDER MANAGEMENT

What is Stakeholder Management?

Stakeholder management is a key part of being a Sponsor. It is also one of the most challenging parts because the term is so wide. Stakeholder management is about figuring out who is likely to be impacted by or interested in a project and figuring out how you might encourage them to act in a neutral or supportive way for the project and reduce any negative impacts.

The next step is learning about those stakeholders, understanding what is important to them, and managing the influence and impact that they have on the project.

On large or complex projects it may be that you work closely with other teams such as the Project Management, Sales and Marketing, Operations, and Communications teams to agree on who manages each stakeholder as they may have existing ongoing relationships that they already have to manage. Your focus is on strategic stakeholder management.

Why Stakeholder Management Matters

Stakeholder management matters to Sponsors because it has a significant impact on project success. We are delivering projects in an age where we can perform feats of engineering at high levels of precision and ingenuity. It may take a combination of time and brilliant teams to conquer the technical challenges, but they are rarely the area that derails a project as impactfully as stakeholders.

Stakeholders can have the power to change, delay or cancel your project. Sometimes they may do it actively and consciously and sometimes it may happen through nothing more than their apathy about your project.

Stakeholders with high levels of power and influence need very active management and this isn't something you can expect the project team to manage in totality. Highly engaged supporters can become your biggest asset or your biggest thorn in your side. This could be individuals or groups.

> "Never doubt that a small group of thoughtful, determined citizens can change the world; indeed it is the only thing that ever has."
>
> MARGARET MEAD

A useful methodology in stakeholder management is stakeholder mapping. This exercise helps you map out the stakeholder by the levels of interest and influence they have and then plan how you manage them accordingly.

Stakeholder Mapping

Use this model to put each stakeholder into one of the four types and then plan your stakeholder management action based on the corresponding advice.

High Influence Low Interest	High Interest High Influence
Type: Influential stakeholders who could have an impact yet are not well-informed or engaged	Type: Influential stakeholders who could have an impact and are well-informed or engaged
Action: Build relationships, engage, or raise awareness to promote influence or prevent negative impact.	Action: Build a relationship, actively manage, and plan frequent engagement to harness support and minimise negative impacts
Low Influence Low Interest	High Interest Low Influence
Type: Stakeholders with little relevance to the team or project.	Type: Stakeholders who could have a limited impact yet are well-informed or engaged.
Action: Be aware of whether any of these could change position at a later stage. Keep informed.	Action: Monitor and engage to watch for changes and ask for advocacy.

This is an important exercise to carry out at the start of a project and to revisit at relevant periods as the views, power, and influence of stakeholders can change over time. They may also change according to the stage of the project.

For example, a particular person or group may not be interested in the idea or concept stage of your project as they don't even believe it will happen. When it has a plan and funding it may suddenly start to pay attention either to support or sabotage. You must be already thinking about which way they may go.

What Sponsors need to know about it

You need to know whether you are good at stakeholder management. It is an area that you can continuously develop throughout your career as a Sponsor and still feel like you are gaining from the time invested in learning and improving.

Are you a great stakeholder manager? I heard a Head of Sponsorship describe great Sponsors as chameleons. Ask yourself if you are a chameleon or if you are good at getting on with people who are like you or whom you have a natural affinity with.

How do you get on with people who are so unlike anyone in your circle? Do you strive and stretch and adapt yourself to find a way to build rapport, relationships, and understanding with them? Or do you allocate management of them to someone else which means you don't have to deal with them? It is certainly a way of managing a challenging stakeholder but by doing so you miss the opportunity to hone your skills and move from good to great.

We don't like everyone; we are tribal and commonality can be a good ground for relationships. Instinct can also be good at getting us away from people who are toxic to us. In a professional environment as a Sponsor, we simply don't have that luxury.

We do have a responsibility to create as positive a relationship with every stakeholder we are managing as possible.

Types of Stakeholders

Campaign groups

Campaign groups are generally filled with passionate people. Highly engaged supporters can become your biggest asset or your biggest thorn in your side. Many infrastructure projects attract campaign groups who either championed the idea of the project or helped push political will over the line. Or campaign groups who do not want the project to go ahead or want it amended in some substantial form.

Sponsors can harness this power to help drive the project forward if it is a supportive campaign group. They should also be aware that these types of groups can often feel a high sense of ownership of the project and may seek a more influential role. Balancing the help without losing control of the project is a delicate line and one that Sponsors should take care to manage.

When the campaign group is opposed, the Sponsor must be aware of them and have a plan to manage their opposition. Overlooking a stakeholder's needs and impact can also have a detrimental impact on a project.

There was a major project which was struggling to secure its next stage of funding. The Sponsor advised that all relationships were good and that they had a good insight into how all of the relationships with stakeholders were functioning. It became clear from speaking to others on the project and the stakeholders that the relationships were good with all of the people who were similar in personality style, background, professional experience, and demeanour to the Sponsor. They spoke highly of the Sponsor and were aligned with their objectives and vision.

Outside of that group were individuals who felt marginalised, unheard, and devalued. The Sponsor was concerned with figuring out why the project wasn't gaining support for its next stage of funding and spending time trying to mitigate it by explaining the benefits and business case over and over.

That was not the problem. The people who had the power to progress the points understood them. They just didn't feel bought into this project. Upon asking them what was happening they explained that felt that when they spoke to the Sponsor they were patronised. The Sponsor spoke to them in a way they felt implicated that if they were smarter they could make better arguments on behalf of the projects to unlock the money.

They had multiple competing priorities for the funding all of which had good business cases and benefits. As a stakeholder group, they were blocking this project with the powerful tool of inertia.

They understood implicitly that no decision is a decision in itself and refused to accelerate or lobby those with the money on their behalf. They passed on reports and memos and turned up at committee meetings. What they did not do was be vocal, lobby, and take all the extra subtle actions needed to get the funding through.

Put yourself in the Stakeholder's shoes

Whilst Nelson Mandela was imprisoned on Robyn Island, he knew that if he wanted to influence or change the minds of the white Afrikaners who ruled South Africa with an oppressive regime of Apartheid that he had to start by understanding their current mindset. He talked about not being able to negotiate until he made the changes to himself first.

This was stakeholder management at its most extreme and with the highest prized outcomes attainable. The freedom of a people. So he watched and he learned and he did all he could with his limited access to resources to get inside the mind of the white South African ruling class. He knew for example that they watched a lot of rugby, and it was treated with cultural reverence. He watched hours and hours of rugby purely with the purpose to try to look through their eyes.

What Nelson Mandela tells us is relevant to stakeholder management. Once you understand the perspective of a stakeholder you are in a far stronger position to understand their views, needs, objections, desires, and even their support for your project.

Resources to understand your External Stakeholders

It has never been easier to get access to information. The plethora of published words opens a world of opportunity for the Sponsor seeking to understand their stakeholders better. The trouble is no longer the dearth of information but information overload -what to read, how much, reliability of sources all compounded with the balance of keeping the day job going make it challenging.

Here are some ideas as to how to target your efforts best and streamline your research to gather really useful information on your stakeholders.

This looks at stakeholders who are most likely to be external to your organisation but perhaps not your industry. The importance of understanding your own business and the needs of internal stakeholders are discussed next.

Public Sector

If you are working within the public sector, there are some key sources that you want to mine. Major Projects are often funded by central government and can be anything from overhauling the health service, and IT systems and relocating government functions to small and major infrastructure projects.

It's important to understand the structure of the department and the 'who's who'. This is likely to be published on their website with a history of the individuals. Use this to understand what the roles mean and who does what.

There is a major difference between members of the civil service such as permanent secretaries and department directors and members of government such as ministers and their advisors. The difference is that members of government are elected representatives who are there to set policy based on the will of the people who elected them as outlined in their political manifesto and campaign promises. The role of the civil service is to implement that policy regardless of whether they agree with it as they are a politically neutral part of the government. Whilst politicians are elected and can change at a variety of times the civil service remains in place to provide consistency in running the various departments that any country needs to function. This is true of the UK, Australia, Canada, and the US where the terminology may change but the division between government departments and government exists in a similar format.

If your project is government funded you will have a relationship with the government either with politicians, the civil service, or both. How direct often depends on the profile of the project and the seniority of the Sponsor. Your organisation may have people in-house who are there to help you understand the political context, provide briefings or help you manage the relationship. If you have this support, it is very useful to make as much use of that as you possibly can.

Government-funded projects are subject to enormous political pressure and impact, the more you arm yourself with knowledge about the risks and opportunities the more able to protect and manage your project you will be.

You can easily see who the Minister or Member of Parliament is for any key department that is funding or involved in your project. You may want to look at their webpage to understand their key priorities. If the governing party has an election manifesto that includes your project then you should recognise that as crucially important to them as a government. You may even get to Sponsor a project with cross-party support. Somewhat of a unicorn but not entirely unknown.

You will then be able to find all of that information from one of two sources. Either you have a public affairs team in-house or a contract with a firm to provide you with that or you do your political research. Look at the minister's web page. Seek out news articles giving their party's position on the project or project outcomes or look in the manifesto.

Whose idea was it and what stage of the political cycle you are in can also have a significant impact on projects and you should learn what these impacts are. Very often the civil service teams are excellent guides to this as they will live and breathe it all of the time. They may not have mentioned it because they may assume that the knowledge is common knowledge, so it is always worth asking them.

Private Sector

If you are sponsoring a project funded by a private company that you work for you should have access to a significant amount of information. This along with your knowledge and experience of working there forms the basis of your internal stakeholder research.

If you are sponsoring a project on behalf of a private company that you are not employed by you will be best to start doing some research. Go well beyond the blandness of a simple Google search and look at the company's website. The 'about us' section might be the least clicked on part of their website but it is likely someone took the time to write down what they are about, some of their core values, and the foundation of their business.

If you take an interest in learning about the company and its objectives from a corporate level first it will make it easier to understand the context of the project's objectives when building a relationship with people who work for and with them and manage their needs as a stakeholder. It will at least save you embarrassment at a later stage when they reveal something that creates a fundamental flaw in your stakeholder management planning.

Trade Press

You may not be that interested in the latest technology advancement in the industry but if your stakeholder is then it is your job to at least know their industry context. Trade press is a great insight into any industry and is generally relevant and current. A few issues of some good trade press might save you hours of research into the industry. A bonus is that much of it is free as it is funded by advertisers. Have a look online to sign up or glance at the nearest coffee table in your stakeholder's office or in this age of hot desk buildings whatever space was formerly known as a coffee table!

Internal Stakeholders

Industrial relations

Industrial relations depend on your industry and the country you work in. In the UK you will need to know whether trade unions are recognised by the employer, and you should at least factor in an early discussion with your HR department to ascertain whether your project is likely to have any industrial relations impact.

In America and Canada, you will need to know if any changes or the project itself impacts any roles that are union roles. You will need to understand whether the roles affected are union jobs or not. If they are classified as union jobs then all staff in those roles are union members. If the jobs are non-union then no one in those roles is a member of a trade union.

If you are sponsoring a business change it would be wise not to assume that what you think is an improvement will be universally welcomed and embraced by all as such. Missing out on the impact of any industrial relations issues could lead to unwelcome costs, delays in re-work, or potential industrial action. It may be that it could be easily avoided by early consultation and giving the trade union members the option to help shape or inform your project choices at an early stage. It may also help you rule out options if you have a feasibility stage as they are likely to be quite vocal about which options can be negotiated and which are not even open to discussion or are part of wider collective bargaining discussions which you will need to know whether you can move into that territory before proceeding.

It is at your peril that you overlook the trade union or go to see them without including your human resources team. Maybe you want to know their stance on certain issues before you go to see them. That can be easy, read their bulletins on their website, speak to your Human Resources industrial relations specialist, or have a discussion with your trade union representatives, facilitated of course by your Human Resources team.

Managing Stakeholders when you don't love the project

In Samuel Coleridge's Ancient Mariner, the old sea dog of the title kills an albatross that is following his ship. The ship suffers a series of terrible events and the entire crew blames it on the Ancient Mariner and his killing of the albatross. He is made to wear it around his neck in penance for his dreadful deed.

References to this tale may seem better placed in a book on poetry instead of a business book on sponsorship. At some point in your career as a Sponsor, you will get an albatross. Not an actual massive wing-spanned dead bird strapped around your neck but a metaphorical albatross. A project albatross. One that feels like penance, a horror of a project. Your reason for feeling that way could be any number of reasons.

It can be a challenge here if you want to be congruent and genuine whilst acting as an ambassador for the project when you don't want to be sponsoring it. The good news is you can do both. You are a professional being paid to do a job so there is an element of getting on with it. There is another option too.

Search within it for something that you love about this

project. Find something, someone, or some part of it that appeals to you. Dig deep if you have to and use that as your foundation to build your enthusiasm for the project. Start with the benefits. Are they worthwhile, do they add something to people, places, or the world that is in some way positive? What about the location or the technology or the people you will be working with? There will be something, somewhere that you can find the good in and focus on to help you feel more motivated about promoting this project.

When sponsoring rail projects, I did a lot of community events. At times these were very challenging. Linear construction projects can be very difficult for the communities who have to live alongside them during the construction phase. These community events were important for me as Sponsor to attend and talk to impacted neighbours, explain why we were doing the project, when we would be doing certain works, and what we would be doing to minimise impact. At times I would end up doing them as an apology tour for errors or disruption. One of the best facets of these though was to get to talk to people who would be the eventual beneficiaries. You may wonder why not use the word passenger well that is because not everyone who benefited from the railway being built would be a passenger.

Some people were looking forward to using the train, others talked to me about the stations bringing people into their business and some about their teenage children being able to access education and leisure without them having to act as their taxi drivers. They were looking forward to a Friday night with a glass of wine instead of a chauffeur's hat.

These chats helped serve as reminders about why we were doing it. That anticipation of the benefits made the challenges worthwhile. It also gave deep insight into what mattered to stakeholders and how we could manage the messaging during any disruption.

Stakeholder and bad news

No one likes to tell or hear bad news. It is an inevitable and uncomfortable part of project life that Sponsors have to deal with. You owe it to your project and your stakeholders to do this task with integrity and confidence.

Is there anything happening this year that could impact a stakeholder's view of your project? Whether positive or negative make sure you know, diary the event or milestone and check in with them around this time. Is there a time they are really busy? Put that in the diary too and show that you respect their priorities.

A great tip from a Sponsor in one of our training sessions recently was that if he wanted to float a new idea with his line manager, he had noticed that she was more receptive on a Thursday than on Mondays so he planned around that. Whilst the explosive type of bad news that is going to hit tomorrow's headlines cannot be delayed you may know when is a good time or even a good environment to share the news.

I once had a client who was explosive if you told him anything vaguely sounding like bad news in front of his team. Get him alone and he was ok. He would ask questions and explore rather than explode. His ability to respond rather than react was significantly impacted by the presence of other people. Accepting that and making sure to grant him that privacy anytime bad news had to be shared was an easier piece of stakeholder management planning than trying to change his behaviour.

Top Tips for sharing bad news with stakeholders

Have a strategy

Clients and funders like to hear first. Boards and executive committees should also hear from you before someone else tells them. Consider who else needs to know. You need to plan what you are going to say, whom you tell, in what order, and when. A good stakeholder management plan should already be in place giving you a useful starting point.

Be open and authentic

Talk about what has happened truthfully. Avoid spin and jargon. If there are confidentially issues tell people that. Share what you are permitted to do and confirm when you can share more details.

Acknowledge their emotion

If you are sharing bad news with any stakeholder, it is because it impacts them. They may be angry, upset, disappointed, afraid, or shocked. Be understanding, don't take it personally, and allow them time and space to deal with that. Not everyone can move straight to recovery mode.

Take courageous action

Once you have a strategy, start to talk to people. Delays may waste time for mitigation plans or controls to be put in place. It will certainly irritate stakeholders if they feel you put off telling them. The most important characteristic of a Sponsor is integrity. It will shine through when you are courageous on those tough days you have to share bad news.

3

MANAGING CHANGE

What is managing change for Sponsors?

Sponsors drive the change from an existing state to a future state on behalf of a business, a funder, or a client. They often use a project to create change and deliver the desired benefits. They balance the need to lead a strong process with demonstrating exemplary behaviours.

Nowhere is that needed more than leading teams and companies through the process of change throughout the development and delivery of projects. Change, however practical and technical the change is, creates an emotional reaction in people due to how it impacts individuals on a neurological level.

The brain's job is to keep the body alive. This is sometimes described as the brain's job being to keep the body safe.

Brains are far more complex than that. If the job was to keep the body safe it would logically follow that the brain would guide you to a situation of safety over one of danger. That's not the case.

The brain figures out what you can survive, and the neural pathways developed to stay there, knowing that you can survive there is far stronger than any desire to move to a safer situation. Simply put this is because what may be safer is not yet proven to your brain. Thus, it will not drive you to an unknown situation with a potential for greater safety over the known ability to survive.

Knowing that everyone is hard-wired to resist change even when it may be beneficial to them is a fundamental psychological starting point for Sponsors to understand when managing change. When you are leading people into the change you are therefore leading them into ambiguity. Our brains do not like ambiguity one bit. It could be dangerous. There could be sabre tooth tigers.

Remembering as you try to drive change that even your project's biggest supporters have brains that are unconsciously against change helps depersonalise some of the inevitable resistance to change you will experience.

Why it matters?

You must understand that you are leading a process of change filled with ambiguity and take time to understand how that might manifest itself in people's actions, thoughts, feelings, and beliefs.

Without the change, your project is trying to achieve being successful the benefits are unlikely to be delivered and that is a key part of the role. It is all the elements around the change that if not corralled and managed can lead to the dilution, non-delivery of, or disappointment in the benefits that chief executives are talking about in their replies to surveys about projects.

When projects come undone spectacularly it is rarely the technical aspect. It is far more likely to have been a result of resistance to change or rejection of too much ambiguity by stakeholders. To avoid this, you need to strategically plan how you will manage the change in all aspects including the psychological impact of the change.

Great sponsors make this look easy. How do they achieve this when everyone knows that change management is hard? They do it with the grace of a swan gliding on the surface and the hard paddling going unnoticed beneath the surface. They start from an understanding of the psychological impact of change as a necessary insight to be successful in change management and sponsorship. There are several models and theories along with many excellent books on change management.

For insight into what is happening to people during change, a good one is the DREC curve. This is based on the work of

Elizabeth Kubler-Ross studying people responding to terminal illness diagnoses.

The DREC curve is a simplified version of her Kubler-Ross Curve, commonly used to describe reactions to change outside of the medical arena. The diagram below shows the DREC Curve.

THE CHANGE CURVE

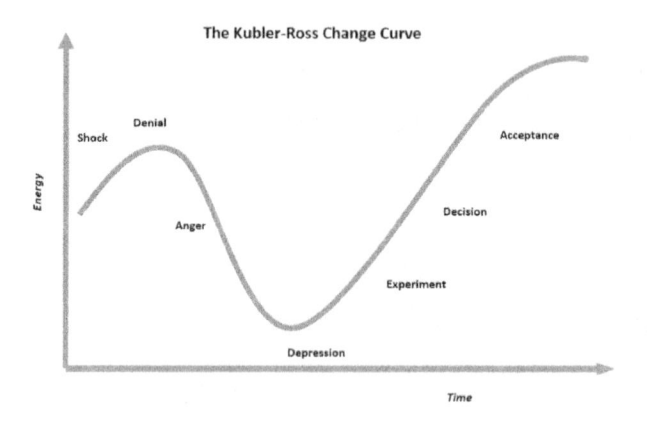

The Kubler-Ross Change Curve — Shock, Denial, Anger, Depression, Experiment, Decision, Acceptance (Energy vs Time)

Applying this to a Sponsor leading change we can consider the DREC curve in the four phases people move through during change.

Denial Phase

This is the initial phase and is around not accepting at all the change proposed or the need for change.

What you might hear:

- We don't need to change.
- It works fine.
- We've always done it this way.
- Silence.

What you might see:

- Non-attendance at meetings and briefings.
- Unopened or unread emails about the change.

What you might experience:

- Lack of engagement in briefings.
- Refusal to engage.
- Feelings misaligned with others.
- Beliefs from others that this simply won't happen.

Resistance Phase

Now that it is clear that you are thinking of going ahead with this change it is time for the resistance to begin. This can take many shapes and forms.

What you might hear:

- I support the idea but...

- You will never get agreement from operations/consenting agencies/individuals/unions
- We tried that before and it didn't work.
- I don't support the idea because...
- It cannot be done.
- It should not be done.
- My job will be harder.
- My job will no longer be required.
- I don't understand what is in it for me.

What you might see:

- Counter briefings.
- Outraged response.
- Passive aggressive responses.
- Passive resistance.
- Aggression.

What you might experience:

- Groups and factions form with similar objections.
- Friction.
- People go above or below your grade to subvert your actions.
- Active sabotage of your plans.
- Feeling isolated as you become the personified representation of the change to those resisting.
- Anger towards you.

This is the most challenging and emotive phase of the change. It is during this phase that even some of those you had in your stakeholder management plan as high influence, high-interest supporters of your change start to show some resistance. Remember that a lot of it is being driven by their unconscious and that this phase is inevitable, uncomfortable, and something you have to help them navigate as a Sponsor.

Exploration Phase

This is the phase when people have moved on from hoping it won't happen, trying to stop it and accepting that this change is likely to happen so how can they best accommodate it into their own life and world.?

What you might hear:

- It could work for me if you include or exclude...

- If this were to happen...
- If this was to work it would ...

What you might see:

- Bargaining with you.
- Bargaining between groups.
- Gradual softening of resistance.

What you might experience:

- Negotiation tactics are being used.
- Modifications to the change being proposed.
- New groups forming.
- Genuine issues are being raised for you to consider.
- Relief!

This is essentially a negotiation phase for a sponsor. Be honest and realistic about what you can add, accommodate or accomplish. Over promise and you will either add to your scope or fail to deliver. Fail to resolve and you will create barriers for the future or risk being stuck in this phase. Where Sponsors can add value at this phase is resolving the competing demands during the exploration phase. More on this later.

Commitment Phase

What you might hear

- Ok, I'm in.
- I can see this working.

What you might see:

- Mobilisation of support.
- People taking action.

What you might experience:

- Support.
- Encouragement.
- People acting like it was their idea all along!

Once you get people to the commitment phase you must follow up on your promises, and commitments and communicate changes. Sometimes things happen that create changes on the project that may impact people or groups whom you have worked with to get them to a place where they committed to the change. This is when you have to revert to them and be open about what those changes mean to them. Fail to do this and you risk the success of the project and will have no credibility to influence those people in the future.

I considered for a time if the best Sponsors are those who are most comfortable with change as everything we do as Sponsors is driving change. I believe that it is the case that those Sponsors who best understand change and how it impacts individuals and groups and can help others navigate it calmly are the most effective.

Using the DREC curve gives a somewhat simplified view for ease of understanding a framework you can apply in your planning and experience. The reality is that this process is not always linear. People move at different times through the phases. Sometimes events occur or information becomes available that puts people back a phase. It also overlooks those people who feign commitment but who are so deeply entrenched in resistance that they become the fifth column.

Planning changes that Alter Operations

Part of your research phase of managing change has to be understanding the current state, and how it works or doesn't work for the people involved. When you are planning a project which makes a change to the current operational state you must spend time mapping out how that might affect those people or groups and how they might perceive it whether that be positively or negatively.

Put yourself in their shoes as much as possible and look for all the positives and negatives that you might have to talk through with them. If you avoid the negatives completely it will look like you don't understand their point of view or that you are guilty of the sins of oversimplification or optimism bordering on naivety. High-performing conversations include being able to talk about difficult and negative topics without asking others to suspend their emotions.

Your enthusiasm for delivering the benefits is a brilliant strength if you have a natural charisma that can be infectious and will help you get people on board with your change. There are times when you need it in equal measure with self-awareness though. You may need to deal with people who are very adversely affected by your project and in that case, you need to temper your enthusiasm with humility and respect for their circumstances.

Often overlooked is to need to plan and allow for time for Sponsors to understand the existing state in a sufficient level of detail. It is not planned because it is often not valued highly enough. Without exception, every sponsorship role can be made easier or more efficient by a thorough understanding of the existing state. It is useful to know why it is important, how to efficiently create that understanding, and how to leverage it for successful outcomes.

If we look at the Sponsor's role in the change we see that they have to be ambassadors for that change. They are there to extol the virtues of the future state but that must of course be relative to the existing state and take account of the strengths and weaknesses of the existing state.

Existing state means where we are now in terms of the operations of the whole business and/or the part that the project is being done to or for. The future state is where we will be after the change.

It is important to understand the difference between where the existing state would be without the project in any situation where the project must happen as a result of legislative, logistical, mandated, or practical situations. This is because people may not know or understand that the existing state cannot continue in its current form.

If this is the case then it is important to be open about this and it should form part of your communications and stakeholder management plan. It becomes how you answer some of the 'why should we bother' questions from detractors. A case in point is hospital upgrades in the UK. In the UK many hospitals were built in the Victorian era (1837-1901) or earlier. They were built when medicine and health care were at rudimentary stages. Treatments were not always sophisticated nor was the equipment used to diagnose or treat people. Fast forward to the modern day and we have moved on immensely in both our understanding of the body as a system and our ability to create technology that diagnoses and treats illness. When these hospitals were built they did not anticipate that instead of doctors tasting urine (yes really) to diagnose kidney problems they would now use an MRI machine which also diagnoses many other illnesses. The doctors who were specialists in urine tasting often called

Water Testers would have weighed around 80kgs. An MRI machine weighs between 4500kg-16,000kgs. Quite the leap in logistics as well as medical advancement. Many of the UK's historic hospital buildings quite simply were not built with rooms with space to install modern-day equipment or floors strong enough to support their weight. These often cannot be viably adapted to hold lifesaving equipment. Building modern hospitals which can accommodate these have often been the only realistic answer. Many of the hospitals demolished were ones that the public already knew were becoming increasingly challenging to maintain, clean, and prevent the rapid spread of infection within. The resistance to change still happened though and campaigns with nostalgic, emotive overtones grew rapidly.

Sponsors leading the projects to build new super hospitals and demolish historic assets have often met significant resistance to this change. Being very clear in their messaging that the alternative is neither viable nor palatable has helped them move dissenters through the DREC curve. They used clear simple messaging designed not for clinical practitioners or those working with the built environment but for the average member of the public.

The narrative and debate did move to how they were funded as many of the new hospitals were funded as a part of Private Finance Initiatives, the same concept as Public Private Partnerships.

This move from debating 'should we do this' to ' how should this be funded' is a classic move from resistance to the exploration phase of change in the DREC curve.

Taking people with you through a clear narrative of how, why, what, where, and when, starts with a recognition of your stakeholder's understanding and current knowledge cannot be undervalued.

A major IT project is a good example of this. Not many relish a major IT upgrade, the dreaded migration, or even a new hardware rollout. Attendance at an IT briefing in a large company performed by some very smart, polished, and enthusiastic people left a divided audience behind at the end. Some had no idea what was happening. Some thought new laptops. Some thought IT upgrade. Some had commenced a nice nap as the phrase 'endpoint detection' floated from the podium. A small minority knew what was to happen. They explained it in water cooler chats to

the baffled others in the weeks to come afterward. No one was getting a new laptop. Four things were happening:

- Everyone in the company is getting an upgrade of the software on their laptop.
- Everyone would have to hand in their laptop for 24 hours for this to happen.
- There would be new features when returned. Some of these would be unseen and undetectable to users, others would be.

- A large amount of data would be moved to cloud-based storage including archived emails.

They knew what would happen and had an outline of when. But why? Chaos reigned supreme. Where there is a lack of clarity and information rumours, and supposition will always fill that void.

What had gone wrong was that the team leading the change had assumed that the knowledge level across the company concerning IT was far higher than it was. They had carefully planned and well executed their plan with admirable enthusiasm. The flaw was their base assumption was wrong from the outset. Everyone might have had a company laptop and could carry out their work on it. Everyone did not understand how that laptop functioned, its relationship to the wider IT system, and its interplay with cyber security, server capacity, and at a basic level that laptops don't live forever!

Working with that team, as they introduced Sponsorship to their projects and looked at lessons learned it became clear that the Sponsorship of that IT project had been added to the work of some of the business analysts rather than as a stand-alone role. They had chosen the best business analysts. Those who had great enthusiasm people skills and technical ability. They had been given no support for stakeholder management, sponsorship, or benefits management.

The IT project team's perspective was: a dream project.

Why were people so unappreciative of the work that went into making this a well-managed upgrade? The majority of outages had been at night, the IT teams had phased the migration so that one team at a time handed in their laptops and got them back twenty-four hours later. That part had all gone to plan. No small achievement with 30,000 laptops.

The technology had all worked. There was online training to teach people to use the cloud storage and teams of people walking the floors for weeks giving support in person. Cyber security had been maintained throughout. The backup servers rented had allowed for a seamless transition with no impact on the operational business. That was a major success as the company run critical national infrastructure. A dream IT project execution.

The stakeholder view was: a disaster project.

Entire teams had no laptop for twenty-four hours which meant everyone with access to secure electronic storage files could not access them. Customers asked for information during that time could thar not be accessed. It rendered whole teams useless for twenty-four hours. Some had been pressured by unscrupulous managers into using a day's annual leave to not be seen as wasteful or inefficient. People had been due to deliver presentations on their hard drives that disappeared into a cloud. Designs and contracts to be issued were also suddenly in the cloud. Service delivery times could not be met. Line managers had to plan for teams to hand over laptops in a phased way adding more work to their day.

Both perspectives are valid. Two different truths can exist in situations such as these. The facts remain the same however, the perception shift is what creates two versions of the same event. This is a fact of life for Sponsors. Whilst you cannot eradicate this you can take action to minimize it happening in your project. You can also learn to accept that sometimes you will try your best and a stakeholder will have the perspective that it simply wasn't enough.

Back on the IT project looking at the lessons learned and helping them reflect on the difficulties they experienced during the rollout phase it became clear what had gone awry.

Tracing the project back to its origins the reasons for the change had never been communicated. The majority of stakeholders, anyone who used a laptop which was around 80% of the employees of the workforce in the tens of thousands, felt that they had been inconvenienced and there was no benefit to them whatsoever. They had been to numerous briefings, had to manage workloads around the need for planned outages, had felt confused, inept, misled, and had upset customers.

Very few of them had any idea why this project had been initiated in the first place. No one had told them what would have happened if they hadn't performed this major upgrade. The IT systems would have been unable to keep performing in the same ways as before. The company servers were groaning under the burden of storing so much information including the literally millions of emails of people who were not following the IT policy and were not deleting or archiving emails or files properly.

The whole system was slowing down, they couldn't just keep adding servers. They were also operating on outdated software. In a few years, everyone would have had issues with essential business such as viewing and editing designs and drawings.

A key element of the upgrade was also cyber security. Hackers were becoming ever more sophisticated not only at phishing scams but also at finding ways into their systems. Not upgrading could have led to issues of national security. They would have become more and more vulnerable.

In a nutshell, without the upgraded IT, like any asset not renewed or maintained its performance would slowly deteriorate until it no longer functioned. They simply hadn't told their stakeholders this at the briefings. Some of the cyber security detail were highly confidential but this wasn't why they didn't tell them. They didn't tell them because they assumed they already knew. They assumed that everyone being onboarded into the business operation was trained in using laptops, understood the implications of breaching IT policy, and that the current state of operations included a high level of IT competency. There was no way of knowing whether it did or not as IT competency was not measured. If they had understood the operation of the business they would have had a deeper understanding of the challenge they were facing in moving people through a significant change.

Of course, the employees didn't know all this about IT. Some did but it was not ingrained corporate knowledge. Whilst the IT team had understood the current state in technical terms, they had not considered the current state of people's understanding. In an organisation this is critical. What is the stakeholder's understanding and view of the current state and how does that correlate to the impact on them about the change? Crack this and you have a far easier road ahead.

At the different stages of change and projects the Sponsor has to manage the ambiguity and the impact that creates on teams, individuals, and the project. At times your role will be to turn that ambiguity into certainty. At times your role will be to help others understand that the ambiguity must exist for longer and help them get comfortable with that. You might do that by guiding, helping, comforting, clarifying, empathising, listening, or offering strategic or tactical solutions. These might be the big as well as the small.

Ambiguity is particularly prevalent during the early stage of a project and during project change.

At the idea or concept stage when an organisation is wrestling with a problem and considering asking a Sponsor to take it forward, this is often peak ambiguity. It may be a stand-alone project or projects which are part of a programme or elements of a major business change that the Sponsor is going to be asked to lead. At this stage, the Sponsor can add value by helping explore the idea. This is a viability stage in advance of feasibility. There will be so much ambiguity that often it can be tempting to dismiss the idea outright at this point. The Sponsor can usefully help categorise which areas of ambiguity don't need to be resolved at this time and which do to move from wondering whether the idea is viable to is it feasible.

Important questions to explore in the early concept stages are:

- Why do we want to do this? Ask why five times.
- Can it be done now?
- What would have to change for it to be possible?
- Is that in our control?
- Is that something we can influence?
- Can we or someone else afford to pay for it?
- What is this about?
- What are the benefits being sought? This helps clarify if this is a benefit-driven project or just a desire to 'do' 'build' or 'buy'.
- What funding is or may be available? What type of funding does it come with any conditions?
- What is the outcome or change they are trying to create?
- Are there any immediately obvious barriers to that change?

- How does this fit with our organisation's strategic objectives, corporate strategy, and values?
- How does this fit with what our customers, stakeholders, and funders expect of us?
- What impact will this have on our operations now?
- What impact will this have on our operations during the project or change?
- What impact will this have on our operations after and during the project or change?

The Sponsor should highlight significant but not insurmountable difficulties with the change. This forms your very first risk register before you have even commenced formal risk management sessions and planning.

Whether your project is an IT migration, an office move, a reorganisation, or building something there are some commonalities to consider as the Sponsor at the outset of considering a change.

Important questions to explore are:

Do you need someone else at this stage? A project team, development team, change managers, designers, engineers, consultants, technical experts, financing advice, industrial relations expertise?

Should you create a document noting what the business desires and what you as Sponsor require from anyone else involved?

Can you define the client's proposition into outputs, needs, requirements, and outcomes?

Can you investigate the feasibility and potential solutions through to proposing a single option solution?

Have you agreed with your client that you will come back with a recommended single option or more than one?

Are the reasons for discounting or promoting a particular solution being recorded as you proceed? What seems an obvious reason now may get lost in the mists of time if you are challenged later or need to respond to stakeholders or consenting agencies about why you discounted a solution or approach.

Here you are taking the benefits that the client wants and finding ways that deliver them within the parameters of the existing business case. You will of course be developing the fuller or next stages of the business case as you proceed throughout this stage. There is no need to wait until the end of a stage if you find that the business case collapses early on. We will look in detail at what that would look like in Chapter 5 Business Cases.

If what you are seeking is so far beyond the realm of the achievable it is success rather than failure to point out as soon as it is demonstrably beyond a reasonable doubt. This is very different from stopping because it is too hard. If achieving benefits remains your primary focus and driving force, you are doing the job the best way you can. In this way, you can avoid being distracted or set off course by people who have already jumped to the solution. As the guiding mind of the project, it is incumbent upon you to ensure that all options are explored relative to the business case and within the budget available at this stage.

This stage is so formational that it can be filled with ambiguity. The work of getting your stakeholders engaged, your solutions initiated and into development, consents, or technical approval considerations are complex. There are so many moving parts, often paced differently. The hurdles that need to be overcome can be immense. It can be an immense challenge for a Sponsor and the time you add the most value.

Take comfort in the fact that you are working to resolve issues now to avoid solving them in the future when they will cost more, delay or destroy the project or derail the delivery of benefits. Solving the issues of consents, permissions, corporate strategy or strategic fit, stakeholder buy-in, approvals, and understanding stakeholder objections or industrial relations are all far more difficult to solve the further you go into a project lifecycle.

Top Tips for Managing Change

Great Sponsors take care to:

- Understand the current state and strengths and weaknesses of business as usual.

- Impact assess any changes.
- Agree on the future state, scope, and cost envelope.

Future state

Sponsors are accountable for:

- Delivery of benefits.
- The success of the investment.
- Outcomes being achieved as promised.
- Making sure the new operational state works.

Business expectations

Sponsors should lead:

- Journey through change.
- Benefits and business case.
- Governance, assurance, and risk appetite.
- Corporate strategy.
- Stakeholder management.
- Management of ambiguity.

Behavioural expectations

Sponsors should demonstrate:

- Values, culture, and role model behaviours.
- Support for project or change.
- Engagement and best practice.

- Coaching approach.
- Self-awareness.
- Emotional intelligence.

In summary, know what the current state is, know what the change you have to drive is, understand the parameters that you have to drive that change within, and decide how you will behave throughout.

This is a surefire way to set yourself off on the track to being a great Sponsor.

4

BENEFITS MANAGEMENT

What is Benefits Management?

Benefits = Why bother with projects?

Benefits Management is agreeing on what benefits are to be achieved from the investment and project and delivering those benefits. Sponsors drive forward the delivery of benefits. This normally involves a change to the operating environment or the creation of a new operating environment. The Sponsor leads and drives that change throughout.

Why Benefits Management Matters

In 2015 The Project Management Institute, Pulse of the Profession study found that 80% of Chief Executives surveyed stated that they were unhappy with the benefits delivered by the projects undertaken by their teams.

One would be forgiven for thinking that is because those projects were late or over budget. Surprisingly it was the same rate of disappointment in project benefits regardless of whether the project was on time and on budget or not.

This is a sobering statistic. If you are a chief executive, you could be well advised to slash your projects mercilessly. Indeed, why not if only 20% of them are likely to deliver the benefits you want? The statisticians amongst you can calculate what % of projects these chief executives can expect to be successful if you also count on time and on budget as success criteria.

Before we send to hear for whom the bell tolls in this project cull, we could advise the chief executive to instead employ a professional Sponsor. Any Sponsor worth their salt will be adept at benefits management.

Benefits Mapping or Tracking

Benefits Management journey

Managing benefits can be viewed as a journey of the benefits from concept through to operation. A Sponsor needs to know the lifecycle of benefits because apart from some interim benefits most benefits are not delivered until after the project is complete. This is part of the reason a Sponsor often has to be the first person allocated to a project and the last person to leave.

A model we have created for the benefits management lifecycle is:

Identify benefits	Plan to deliver benefits	Map benefits	Track benefits	Realize benefits	Remeasure benefits
Why are we spending money on this?	How will we achieve the benefits we want?	What delivers the benefits we are paying for.	How do we monitor that those benefits are on track to be delivered? What happens to benefits during changes?	Delivery of the whole reason 'why'.	Check and confirm that the benefits delivered match or exceed those predicted in the business case.

You can find a useful graphic and tool for applying this on See Change International's website.

The link between benefits, change, and scope is an area where Sponsors must have a significant depth of understanding. Investing the time, in the beginning, to thrash this out is time well spent.

Useful questions to ask are:

- Have you identified all benefits?
- Which aspects of your scope are fundamentally linked to the benefits?
- How strong is that link?

- If you reduce, remove, or alter the scope what does it do to the benefit and how does that fit with the needs of your client and with other stakeholders?
- How will you track the delivery of those benefits throughout?
- How will you protect benefits during change?
- Have you any lessons to apply from the last time round or the organisation's last project?

Talking about benefits has become popular in recent times in project and investment cycles. There is however still some dubiety as to what that means.

This chapter breaks benefits into categories and talks about each of those generally and then gives examples from different industries.

What are the Benefits?

The benefits can be described as the real reason for the existence of a project. Even if change managers, project managers, and sponsors wake up every day thinking 'I would like to change or build something' funders and clients do not normally commission projects on this basis. Well, not successful ones.

A general principle of projects is that someone is seeking to change something for the better. What better looks like or delivers is often the benefit.

It can get confused with the scope at times. In construction and infrastructure sometimes, people talk about the end product being the benefit. A new road, a new railway a new or upgraded hospital, 800 new homes, a shopping centre, or the world's tallest office block. These achievements may be monumental, inspiring, and great to wrap a ribbon around for an opening ceremony but the end product is not usually the benefit.

The benefits are the results that come from building these new products not the product in itself.

For example, transport projects usually have tangible, directly measurable benefits such as:

- Reduced journey time between points a and b.
- Extra capacity for x number of people to move between points a and b.
- Connectivity between place a and place b.
- Increased access to places of employment and education.
- Increased access to leisure opportunities.

The socioeconomic benefits of such projects are harder to measure but could include:

- Increased social value in areas previously isolated from each other.

- Sustained socio-economic growth in areas with improved transport links.
- Housing growth including new homes or increased housing values (for some this is a disbenefit)

Looking at a different sector we can see how the benefits are described there.

Retail and commercial tangible, directly measurable benefits:

- X no square feet of office or retail space with a rental rate of x£ per square metre.
- X no of jobs created in x area.

Socio-economic benefits

- Improved town centre environment.
- Spur for economic growth in an area.
- May have distinct prestige for those involved in design and construction.
- Prestige and advertising for the local area from iconic buildings.
- Improved levels of personal safety perception.

Business change

The benefits of a business change are generally targeted at either adapting to a changing world or improving business outcomes. An example could be an IT project to educate teams on not clicking unsafe external links in emails so the benefit may be reducing exposure to external threats such as phishing or hackers. It could be implementing the availability of new technology such as video conferencing. Video conferencing is not a benefit in itself. Why have businesses invested in it? Because the benefit is linked to the value of time and also costs. That is time not traveling to meetings and the cost of travel combined with meeting space. This benefit was never appreciated more than during the Coronavirus pandemic of 2020 when much of the world had to stay home and many roles suddenly became home-based and carried out over video.

Generally, business change projects are driven by the same underlying benefits. These are:

- Improving turnover or profitability.
- Increased profit margin.
- Reduced costs or overheads.
- A more efficient and effective way of doing things.
- Increased employee engagement.
- Change in regulation or law.
- A more efficient and effective way of doing things.
  (One without the other won't improve your profits by the way.)

What Sponsors need to know about it

How to get your head around Benefits Management

This is one that Sponsors struggle with across every industry, in every country that we work and in every type of project you can think of. If benefits are the reasons for doing projects then why is it so hard and how can Sponsors find some clarity on how to improve benefits management?

First, the elephant in room, it is hard because it is hard. Sponsorship is a rewarding role and one that makes a huge difference to the projects that often shape the world we live in. It is still important to acknowledge the complexity of the task and one layer of complexity is benefits management.

Benefits management is diverse. The benefits don't always seem easy to align with the scope of the outputs. Some are monetised and some are not. Some are quantitative and some are qualitative. And yet all of them matter. Consider an example of a housing project. If you build houses, you have met the basic benefit of creating places for people to live.

If they are hideous with no public realm and are purely functional you can expect a backlash and some unpleasant headlines because those non-quantifiable benefits of having a nice place to live matter.

Whilst they are harder to measure than the binary point of having a roof over your head they are felt very strongly and everyone can relate to them. Those benefits must be captured as scope or requirements at the outset if you expect to see them delivered.

An engaged Sponsor plans and manages benefits throughout. Never losing sight of the fact that they are the reason for the existence of the project. This will help secure the delivery of the benefits, and perhaps more importantly it will serve you well during change control and during the most valuable work a Sponsor can do which is cancelling the project that won't deliver the benefits. There is more on these in Chapter 5 Business Cases and Chapter 7 Governance.

Top Tips on Sponsor's Role in Benefits Management.

Understand

If your project scope is the 'What' the benefits of your project are the 'Why'. Sponsors own the benefits and are accountable for their delivery. Step one is a thorough understanding of what those benefits are and how they are delivered, realised, and measured.

For every project, a sponsor must know:

1. What are the benefits and whom do they impact?
2. Who does the project impact and what is their benefit to them?

Sensitivity Analysis

Sponsors should understand the sensitivity around the project benefits. What changes are likely to improve or reduce your benefits? If you know this, you are positioning yourself to be able to respond to those changes. The world has a habit of still changing whilst we deliver projects and we must be aware if any of those external changes negate the desire or need for the projects we are Sponsoring, this is particularly true of major and mega projects and IT projects.

Advocacy

Sponsors must promote the benefits of an investment to stakeholders. That takes an understanding of which benefits are relevant to which stakeholders.

Translation

You may want to work with your communications team to help you figure out how to best describe benefits to different audiences especially if some benefits are technical.

5

BUSINESS CASE

What is a business case?

In project terms, a business case is a justification for the project. It usually starts with looking at a problem or strategic need, looking at the potential option to resolve these and the risks involved, balanced against the potential cost and likelihood of a successful return on investment. There are a variety of complex models and methodologies to build and measure business cases. A simple way to consider a business case in financial terms is to think do the benefits of the project outweigh the costs?

This is often taken further and modelled as a Benefit to Cost Ratio (BCR).

The equation for that is:

Benefits divided by costs = Benefit to Cost Ratio (BCR).

How does that work out? If you had a problem that cost £100 and the project was likely to cost £100

Your business case would be:

Benefit £100 divided by Cost £100 = Benefit Cost Ratio of 0

Given that projects can have an element of unpredictable risk and disruption attached it would make no sense to make that investment. Sponsors have to understand the balance of the cost: benefit ratio and the difference between cost and value.

The benefits from the project always have to be valued at a higher cost than the project if you want to have a positive business and Benefit to Cost Ratio.

Of course, it can be the case that the business case is positive but the funding available may not stretch. This is where Sponsors start to get into the complex realms of reducing the scope to bring down the costs and seeing what that does to the benefit. This is very iterative work yet important to undertake when the funding does not meet the costs and the organisation still wants to proceed.

That can present a challenge in those projects where, as discussed in Chapter 4, the benefits are less tangible, and perhaps the value is in socio-economic benefits. There are several business case models now built which allow a value to be attached to these socio-economic benefits to carry out business cases. It is important to have this information not just to be able to choose whether to fund a project and start it but also to be able to compare the business's case to a variety of options that each project might have. Without that information, Sponsors can find it hard to get a decision-making framework that works when there are different project options in an early phase. The Sponsor ends up at the whim of the most powerful voice in a steering committee or the highest presence in political terms. Even with a business case, this can happen, without one it is almost certain.

A trick is not to get lost in analysis paralysis but rather to use business case methods and modelling to help make informed decisions. In reality, we all make business case decisions in life regularly. How often are you faced with a choice of what you want to buy versus the price and can make a quick decision based on what's important to you? We can still use that decision-making ability when the benefits so obviously outweigh the costs or implications of doing nothing.

Why do business cases matter?

Sponsors own the Business Case

Sponsors in the public sector find frustration in having to navigate the rules, paperwork, and business case modelling to get their projects funded stage by stage. This is because they are spending public funds and the duty to spend that as wisely as possible and be able to demonstrate decision-making publicly at later stages is demanding.

They wish they worked in the private sector where a board would approve a business case and let them get on with it.

Sponsors in the private sector often have to answer to shareholders or at the very least those who answer to shareholders. Risk pots are tightly controlled and business cases are examined to be clear about how robust they are. The strength of their predictability concerning profit and loss is examined and tested robustly. Funding and announcements are subject to tie in with the release of the share issues, AGMs, statements, and announcements to the stock exchange.

They wish they worked in the public sector where they just have to produce a decent business case and get funding from the government.

The grass often not only looks greener but also looks easier to mow on the other side!

The reality is that Sponsors will always have paperwork, governance, justification, strategic alignment, optioneering, and number crunching to do and justify to someone. You are likely to be heavily involved in creating the business case and then likely to own it throughout. So love it or tolerate it you may as well get familiar with it and get on with it.

If you are dependent on any department approvals such as funding, business case approval, or consent then you should seek to understand their decision-making process and calendar. Everyone thinks their own project or decision is special (as you should as its ambassador) you should though, realise that central government and corporate functions can be somewhat of a monolith and unlikely to be convening approval committees just for you. Find out their published timelines and add them to your calendar. This way you can track or plan timelines for decisions. I've lost count of the number of Sponsors who advised me that their project was being prioritised only to find them wracked with schedule challenges because it turned out they had to fall in with the same budget cycles as the rest of the project.

If your financial forecasts rarely match your actual financials, you are not on the Christmas card list of whoever is managing the funding being given to your project. Whether that is Treasury, government departments, or a finance team. Especially if your project is being funded with financing or borrowing. This is because you are creating volatility for them in deciding what to borrow and or allocate to you. This means they are borrowing too much cash which they don't use and wastes money. Imagine drawing out cash from your overdraft only for it to sit in your house unspent for you to put it back in the bank next month and pay the interest you now owe.

The opposite is that your overspending creates cash flow crises which have to be solved by shuffling money around departments or additional short-notice borrowing. Either impression it creates is that you cannot accurately plan and forecast how you will spend money. Not a reputation you want.

What do Sponsors need to know about it?

Whilst having a business case framework and parameters to work within can feel constraining to a Sponsor and project team, it is also a vital tool for decision-making. This is especially powerful when events occur that significantly change any of the business case parameters.

Stopping a project using a business case

Stopping a project can be the single hardest task to achieve as a Sponsor.

This may seem strange. After all the knowledge about cost overruns, benefits management, and the growing use and understanding of business cases, gated project management processes surely no project proceeds that shouldn't?

Despite all the aforementioned progress, there are still projects which should have never seen the light of day or should have been stopped when they no longer looked set to be successful or strayed beyond the sensible boundaries of the business case.

Maybe you are working on one of those right now. Everyone is beavering away, burning cash, designing, building, or changing people, processes, or assets. Reports are being generated showing the progress against scope, cost, and schedule. Everything is rosy or maybe even going awry. But you know that this project is in trouble. Maybe it was always in trouble or maybe what started as mildly irritating trouble has grown into a huge bag of worries that you can't escape. You can ignore it, avoid it or pretend you can't feel it. After all, there are probably plenty doing the same around you. For the love of whatever is dear to you STOP IT NOW.

Your biggest project successes as a Sponsor will never be the ones that everyone loves and that you have a clutch of awards for having worked on. That is because the biggest project successes you will have are the ones that you snuff out and stop them seeing the light of day and wasting money, effort, and resources upon.

There are several reasons to stop a project:

- It is now clear that the costs far outweigh the benefits.
- The benefits are no longer wanted, needed, or relevant.
- The technical solution clearly will not work.
- Changes have happened which means it no longer has a viable business case.
- Stakeholders are not going to give you consent to build or operate your asset.
- Change of corporate strategy and the business is no longer supportive.
- No one wants to pay for it anymore.

There is a much longer list of why you might pause a project to consider it, get it into better shape, or let some risks be resolved. The above list and this section are about stopping it to make it stay stopped.

When is enough, enough?

The investment being made on an infrastructure project had a business case benefit of £5.5m. The cost estimated was £7m. Despite having a negative business case a decision had been made, supported all the way to Executive Committee level that the company would make the £7m investment. This was because a life had been lost and a life-altering injury had occurred to another person. The investment being made was to build an asset that would prevent a recurrence of the two accidents by removing the risk altogether. The public outcry and political support for spending more than the business case justified was the reason the company was willing to spend above the business case.

There were a couple of impediments to moving the project from design into construction. One was that the company did not own all of the land required to build the project. The other was that there was a requirement for several mandatory consents from a local authority. Staff at the local authority were coming under considerable pressure from elected local officials either to not grant the consent required or to grant them with increasingly prohibitive conditions.

The challenge of not having the land to build upon nor the consent to build was compounded when the project went out to tender and the tenders returned showed initial costs likely to be more than double the estimate of £7m.

Surely an easy decision to stop the project there and then as the business case was now so poor?

Not quite. It took the support of a line manager, the managing director, the regional head of project delivery, and the economic and safety regulator just to get the idea of stopping it to become part of a dialogue. There was gnashing of teeth, pulling of hair, banging of tables, moody silences, and frank outrage at the prospect of cancelling this project which was on the verge of having a business case of 3:1 that is it would cost £3 for every £1 of benefit.

And that was the best-case scenario because at this stage. It still looked like a fair chunk of that could be spent on the design and development of something that would either never be built or only built after frequent delays and further concessions. All of which would add further to the cost. There was also a view that the work had been put out to tender, and companies had been asked to bid on this work therefore, the additional money must be found, and it should be awarded to someone.

It's worth pausing to think if people would choose to manage their finances this way. You think you might pop a conservatory onto your house. Your neighbour put one on two years ago and it was £3000. You reckon it will cost around £3000 for a nice simple conservatory, maybe a few pounds more for inflation. Then you do some research and realise that your neighbour only uses theirs in summer because in winter it is freezing. Oh, and they mentioned it is a bit damp too.

You have a scope review and decide to add heating to it. You've got a nice gas central heating system running from a modern boiler so shouldn't be too much more, but it does involve an extra tradesman, pipes, water, and radiators. You put your estimate up to £5000. More than you had initially thought and now nearing the top of your budget range. Maybe you can skip a holiday this summer, after all, you will have that nice new conservatory to sit in. You decide to proceed.

You get around three conservatory firms. All are competent, have good history and reputation and you wait for the quotes to roll in. They all mentioned a few issues that you as a layperson had overlooked. Your neighbour had some made ground to put his conservatory on. You have soft ground. Sadly, you forgot about that electricity cable running through the garden out to power your shed. That will need relocating. The conservatory being heated makes it another room in your house. You need planning permission. Which means an architect and drawings and a right to object for your neighbours. The same neighbour whose planning permission you objected to on the grounds it shaded your begonias. Ah, you realise now why their conservatory has no heating!

Also, your access isn't quite good enough for the plant and materials, but the helpful firms have spoken to your neighbour and for a small sum he will let you use his half of your shared driveway.

The central heating presents a little challenge too. Your boiler although fairly new cannot cope with the addition of another room so that needs to be replaced with a bigger boiler. To cap it all the country is doing well, house building is booming, and steel prices are at an all-time high compared with when your neighbour got his installed during a depression.

All told your conservatory can now be built, perhaps next year at a cost of approximately £15000 plus any extra costs not already included for 'unknown utility risks' from moving that cable (oh and add RPI for next year). The great news is you've had a chat with an estate agent and their advice is that a heated conservatory would add around £5000 to the value of your home.

I suspect that unless you have taken leave of your senses or are vastly rich that at this point you descope the heating and buy a portable heater to heat that conservatory or you forget your conservatory plans altogether. So why do talented, professional people not take the same view with project funding? In the case of publicly funded works, they are often still spending their own money. It could be that it is the only project going at the time but in this case, there were more projects than resources to deliver them. No one was going to lose their job.

More likely it was the project phenomenon known as the fallacy of sunk costs. This fallacy decrees that in a Magnus Magnusson-style approach, 'I've started so I will finish' or for those who never watched the BBC quiz show he hosted 'what makes it through feasibility must be built'.

In these cases, Sponsors must imagine themselves in the image of the boy who called out, "The Emperor has no clothes on."

It is down to you and you alone to stop a project which no longer has a business case or will not deliver the benefits desired. Do not go along hoping that spending large sums of money on the construction of assets or edifices, the creation of new technology or gadgetry will somehow make up for a terrible idea. It won't.

We already have enough remains of projects that should never have been built. Somewhere a Sponsor closes their eyes every time they see it because they knew all along it was doomed.

You might find out your project is in irrecoverable trouble through:

- Assurance activities that you or others undertake.
- A major change or event.
- Funding or financing changes.
- Stage gates.

When this happens how do you go about stopping a project? It may be that you are suitably authorised to do so within your organisation. It may be that a sensible discussion with the client talking about what has changed and why you no longer have a viable proposition leads to a closedown of the project or a plan to revisit the previous stage and look at alternative options.

But it might not be that simple. This may be your toughest challenge yet as a Sponsor. It can be said that the best projects a Sponsor does are the ones that don't see the light of day because they shouldn't. They are hard to measure in terms of financial success other than by using the estimated costs avoided. We should not forget the other costs though of potential overruns, waste of the entire budget, reputation, or people's expended effort.

Firstly, you will need a strategy to approach the cancellation of a project. You will need people on your side like never before. You will need personal awareness and resilience. You are embarking on work this is vital yet thankless. No one throws an opening party or puts a ribbon on cancelled projects. You will have to take your joy from the fact that this is good work that you are doing. You will be the hero of your own story, but no one will be reading the book!

You need some tools, and you need data, facts, and analysis. A SWOT analysis is a good tool to use here. It is important to have your facts correct and in order. Make sure that you have done your homework to look at the facts and data from different angles and perspectives. Check that you are seeking evidence and not just seeking evidence to confirm what you suspect or wish to be the truth.

If you are stopping a project for good, sensible reasons then you are far more likely to succeed if you are seen to be presenting a balanced argument that takes account of all facts, even the inconvenient ones.

You may find that people who still want the project to go ahead (try to avoid being frustrated if they were the biggest objectors in the first place) will go around you, above you, push you hard personally and professionally, and undermine you to others. Some very bad behaviour can come into play when you are the force bringing a project to a close. Your only response can be to stay professional. It may feel personal, but you cannot respond in that way. It will test your resilience. The mildest of consolation is that if you never face adversity, you never increase your ability to be resilient.

In the case of the £7m investment that was growing to £14m the backlash from trying to stop the project was severe. People in the project escalated it above the Sponsor only to find that the Sponsor had already briefed upwards to a managing director and executive committee who were supportive of looking for a different way to deliver the benefits. They tried to cut off in-person dialogue with the Sponsor and instead sent very long, formal emails restating their position in a variety of ways. This amounted to 'we should award this contract and hope that you as Sponsor will make miracles happen so these insurmountable problems will disappear, and we can build this thing'

It was clear that this would not happen. The company had been trying to resolve the land issue for ten years. The experience of this local authority was that they were generally reasonable and helpful. If they wouldn't help, it was because they couldn't.

The Sponsor was experienced enough not to believe that somehow so long as the project proceeded towards the construction these problems would be resolved. The project was at an impasse and there was no way through it. There was little option except to abandon the project altogether and look for another way to solve a problem that was still presenting an ongoing danger to public safety. It was time to go back a stage and look for other solutions. The available technology had also moved on at that time and it was time to go back to feasibility and find another way.

Cautionary tale

There is a cautionary tale about applying some very basic business sense to optioneering into business cases. A great example comes from Scotland. A new business which was a large employer was opening a new facility on the outskirts of Glasgow. They needed large volumes of people to work on their premises and their demand for people outstripped the local labour supply.

They knew that they would need to attract people who lived in the city or the suburbs to commute out to their premises. They didn't want everyone driving as they would need to create a big car park that would have made the footprint of their facility too large.

They also had an environmental commitment to encourage employees to walk, cycle, or take public transport to work. They planned for superb cycle storage, showers, and changing facilities. All good there. The challenge was public transport. They were close to a railway line but the nearest train station was just too far away for most people to walk. Even for those who would walk, it was along country roads with no paved footpaths. Not ideal and is simply lethal on dark nights, of which there are many in the West of Scotland. They found within weeks of opening that they were attracting high volumes of people for interviews, but many people were turning down job offers or leaving. The reason was it was too difficult to get to and from work.

So they called for a railway Sponsor to visit them to talk about building a station within walking distance of their premises. The company that owned the railway infrastructure was a different company from that which ran the trains. The helpful Sponsor brought along someone from both companies involved. This facilitated a useful discussion about what could be done to build a new railway station on the existing line within walking distance. The Sponsor explained what would be needed:

Firstly, some early feasibility and business case work. Figure out if there was space in the timetable to stop trains at an extra station on that line. If so would the train operating company be able to stop trains there? Would it require any additional trains or train crew? What were the ground conditions like? Where exactly would the station go? They would have to consider getting power to the station, water, and drainage. It could be a basic station with two platforms and compliant access so either a footbridge or lifts. Who owned the land? It would require a transport analysis, environmental impact assessment, planning consent, a design and development team to look at options, and then a delivery team to build it. Of course, the railway was not funded to build any new stations at will so the company would have to fund it all. The work would also have to be planned around keeping the existing railway running so the end date would take a bit of time to work up.

If they could pay an initial sum to get the project started, then the work to get into contract and do some early feasibility work could kick off as early as three months. Perhaps, if all went well and it was supported by the planning authority a station could be opened in two to three years with trains stopping there. Probably in the region of £3-6million (priced in 2004). The Sponsor was quite pleased with having given a thorough yet simplified explanation of how to build a station on an existing line. They would be happy to work with them to see if they could progress this station idea.

The business development manager from the train operating company listened on. He agreed that if it worked operationally then they would be unlikely to object to an additional station. They would have to be funded for any additional staff and to maintain it but if that was all in order then it seemed a good idea.

The company was beyond shocked. They had assumed that building a station was much simpler. They had thought about a small contribution from them but not millions of pounds and not years. They simply could not operate their business if they could not get staff to and from the building. This was a desperate situation for them.

The Sponsor empathised and said they would as hard as they could but the consent process alone had mandatory timescales which they had to work within.

The business development manager from the train operator had an idea. "You know that as well as running the trains, we also run a bus company?"

"Yes?"

"We could start a bus picking up from the nearest station and dropping them here, take them back in the evening. Just do enough runs to get everyone here. As long as the shifts don't clash with school bus runs we can use those buses."

Seeing light at the end of the tunnel, "When can you start? Please don't tell me two years."

"Monday and the price will be the cost of running it, minus any fares plus 3% profit."

When we live in a world of exciting projects to Sponsor it is easy to forget that some of the simpler solutions can also have the best business cases.

6
SCOPE

What is scope?

The scope of a project is all of the boundaries around a project metaphorically and sometimes literally along with all that has to be done to deliver the benefits. The Sponsor usually sets out a high-level scope at the start of the project and this is clarified in written documents such as the business case. It often evolves into greater detail as the project progresses.

The role of the Sponsor in helping clients define scope is to help them be clear on what is in and what is out of scope. This is to help draw those boundaries around what is required for the project to achieve benefits and what is extra, nice to have, or that old favourite, "You may as well fix that whilst you are there".

Once clear on what is in and what is out of the project scope the Sponsor can work with the project team to protect the scope for there is nothing more certain than at some point someone will wish to add to or alter that scope and then expect no change to delivery times, cost or benefits. That is a mythical unicorn of a scope change. Be excited and take a photograph if you ever see it but do not ever expect it!

A more detailed scope usually comes after harvesting the project requirements. The Sponsor's role in this varies across project types, and industries and what their level of seniority is as a Sponsor.

Some industries turn requirements into scope. Others turn scope into requirements. Sponsors will have a role to play in whichever of those scenarios exist in the project and organisation.

Unfortunately, some companies have no specific policy and both ways happen. This leads to confusion, blurred accountability, and waste. Whichever way is happening where you work you will still have a high-level scope and requirements and/or specifications. It's an ongoing debate but not always a very interesting one.

For simplicity here is a way to look at it

Scope

What is included, desired, and needed? What are the boundaries around that? What is in and what is out?

Requirements

What the stakeholders need or want. The desired outcomes of the projects. This may also include standard or policy requirements and any derogations or special additions. These can be outcome or output based.

An outcome is about the result and output is about the action taken to deliver the outcome. An example of an outcome is improved economic prosperity. An output to achieve that could be a new housing project or railway.

At a micro level, an outcome could be a comfortable place to sit and an output that delivers that outcome could be a bench, seat, or sofa.

Specifications

Specifications are often detailed technical descriptions of how a requirement must be achieved or how it must perform.

A requirement if often the 'what' whilst a specification is the 'how'.

A Sponsor should make themselves familiar with how this terminology is used and planned in their setting. It is worth noting that as project people tend to move around the language and concepts may be used interchangeably and it can be worth clarifying in your project to help keep everyone aligned with what you are doing.

There should always be a clear line of sight between benefits, scope, and requirements, anything that does not fit is potentially extraneous and Sponsors should consider why it is there.

Sponsors may set a high level of scope (what is to be achieved and what to build to achieve that) and have little further involvement beyond governing and assuring that what a project team proposes to do delivers the benefits in the business case and meets the needs of the stakeholders.

The time to get high-level scope correct is at the beginning, time spent agreeing on the boundaries of what is included is never wasted. It can feel like setting boundaries is challenging because there are still high levels of ambiguity at the beginning. However, time spent clarifying what can be refined and agreed upon is worthwhile. This is because the cost of changing scope later in a project, especially during construction is exponentiality higher than at the beginning.

Project budgets are not limitless. Sponsors manage the competing demands of what stakeholders request and business unit requirements in line with the benefits, business case, and affordability constraints. Areas of scope uncertainty need to be resolved by the Sponsor.

Sponsors also have to be the guardian of avoiding things to include, 'whilst you are there...'. Why are these extras being sought? Who is paying? Is the extra time and risk acceptable? Does it still align with the corporate strategy and direction that the company wants?

At least one of the extras that Sponsors are often asked to include unfinished work from a previously incomplete project that has been dumped on an operational department when the time, budget, or energy ran out! It may be that you will include it and that should be a strategic or tactical decision not just blindly folded in.

Requirements management is how you identify, define, agree, record, and deliver the needs of the users and stakeholders for any given project. This is a specific technical skill and competency for Sponsors who work in an environment where Requirements Management is part of their role. It does not apply universally and there are differences in how to best do this according to the industry and project type.

This can be challenging work as you can be subject to power dynamics, turf tussles, technical bafflement, stakeholder emotions, and immovable forces.

Scope, creep, inappropriate change control, and stakeholder disruption at later stages can often come from requests for scope or requirements that were rejected at an earlier stage.

Keeping a record of those and why you accepted or rejected them will help you quickly reassess if the circumstances, budgets, or objectives have changed. It will also help you demonstrate that the choice to not include them was deliberate and not an oversight. It is also good to record corporate knowledge if you move on and another Sponsor takes over.

Even with the nest requirements management and scope planning in the world, there are instances that may necessitate a change to project scope may include catastrophic events, changes in law, or significant safety events or a client changes their mind.

Client-driven scope change

What about when the client changes their mind?

It is important to be clear with the client at any key points that they make scope decisions or choices what the consequences of changing those decisions will be at a later stage. It may be that they simply are not authorised or able to make that choice at the given time. It may be better to pause, however unpalatable that may feel, than to abort or redo work.

Of course, you may do that, and the client may still make a change to the project. Good governance protocol and process should already be in place to help you manage the mechanics of the change but what about the subtle elements? The disheartenment of the project team players, the frustrations of the supply chain, the expectations of stakeholders.

The Scottish Parliament is a well-known project disaster story in terms of cost and programme overruns which the resulting inquiry stated was mostly due to how major scope changes were implemented. Originally estimated at £10-40 million and delivered for £141 million eventually three years late. Beauty being in the eye of the beholder the building is either an architectural marvel or an eyesore. What is without a doubt is that it is a statement building. Built to house Scotland's devolved Parliament in 2004. Devolution took place in 1999 and the elected members of the Scottish parliament, known as Members of the Scottish Parliament (MSP) were temporarily hosted elsewhere in Edinburgh until the new Parliament could be built.

The project to build a new Parliament was mid-construction and the manufacturing of many elements was complete. The project had been subject to many changes that had all added to delays and rising costs. Their biggest was yet to come. One of the key architectural features of the building is the windows. All of the panes of glass were already manufactured and ready for delivery to be installed. On September 11th, 2001, America was the subject of a coordinated terror attack that included the hijack of 2 aeroplanes that were subsequently flown into the twin towers in Manhattan, New York. The aftermath of this tragic event led to rising concerns about security.

This led to a decision to install bomb-proof windows in the Scottish Parliament. The manufactured glass could not be altered so instead all of the windows were abandoned and a new batch was built at a considerable cost and delay to the project. Was it completely unforeseeable? Probably not. Despite a lull in mainland terrorism since the Good Friday agreement in 1998 Britain has long been at threat of domestic and international terrorism. Added to that is the unfortunate fact that elected officials can be seen as targets by those angered by the policy choices or outcomes of the government. Combing these factors sadly you have a group of people arguably in higher need of protection when working in a public building.

Hindsight is 20/20 so it's easy to write now that it should have been foreseeable or that perhaps the spend of millions of pounds of taxpayer's money was wasted, and they should have mitigated the risk another way. However, it is illustrative of the type of monumental and often unexpected change that can be client driven in any project.

The role of the Sponsor is to understand the balance between how the impact of the change on the business case, the benefits, stakeholder needs, and the success of the project. We know from the inquiry that the business case was not rerun in the instance of the Scottish Parliament. We also know that as well as the glass replacement there had to be other internal adjustments to accommodate the different styles and weight of the bomb-proof glass. All leading to the biggest cost rises in the project overall. Perhaps MSPs would have refused to occupy the building without the extra measures and the ultimate benefits would have been lost.

There are times when even the best Sponsor comes up against challenges around scope change that are unsurmountable. For clients, the best we can do is give our best advice. For a project team, the best we can do is explain what and why the change is happening and make sure we secure all of the resources to make the change safely, and ask everyone else to leave them alone to get on with it. We know late change is disheartening for teams, so we have to create an environment that gives them grace during that time.

7

GOVERNANCE

What is Governance?

Sponsors are intrinsic in two types of governance. Project governance and corporate governance.

Corporate Governance

Corporate Governance is the business structure, rules, regulations, procedures, and processes used to manage, control, and direct a company. It will take account of the purpose of the organisation, its legal status, structure, and any regulations and laws in its operational context.

Project Governance

Project governance flows from corporate governance. It is about making sure that the project follows the corporate governance, organisation, and industry rules and procedures at all times. Sponsors must learn to become experts in corporate governance as they will often be accountable for the project governance and for keeping the project compliant with corporate governance.

They will often be discharging those duties on behalf of the board or business.

Why does it matter?

The temporary nature of projects means that at times Sponsors will have to create the structure of the project governance within the existing rules and committees. Creating well-defined governance processes, policies, and structures to drive better outcomes from projects is an important role that a Sponsor can play.

An effective Sponsor will create manageable and effective systematic approaches to controls of decision-making that work with the rhythm of a project to provide careful oversight and decisions within timeframes that don't inhibit progress.

Leading Governance

Good governance structures account for both escalation at appropriate times and anticipate that the extraordinary can, and may, happen. Effective governance takes account of the appropriate level of scrutiny, seniority, accountability, and resource time. On complex projects and programmes, there will likely be hierarchical levels of governance including bodies such as a Project Board.

The role of the Sponsor will often include reporting at various governance meetings or panels that have to be navigated to:

- Secure funding.
- Approve scope.
- Ratify public communication plans.
- Provide updates on progress.
- Report on assurance.
- Manage or approve change control.
- Respond to any crisis.
- Compliance with corporate governance.
- Lead stage gates.

Much of the work of the Sponsor goes into the activity leading up to governance meetings in both getting the information and the stakeholders aligned in advance. Governance panels and committees are often attended by senior individuals. The Sponsor has a dual role in these situations which is to represent the needs of the project and those of the organisation.

Despite creating governance that is purposeful and structured a Sponsor can, at times, find that decisions are being proposed, discussed, and agreed upon outside of these formal arrangements. The formal meetings can be no more than for ratification of decisions that have already happened within other business units or senior groups.

A Sponsor may find themselves delivering a well-rehearsed and meticulously planned pitch on a complex project or stakeholder issues to be met with instant approval and a feeling that the decision had been made before they even started the pitch. The Sponsor may already have known they would get approval from the group because they put in the leg work beforehand that made it easy to have the pitch approved.

Some Sponsors rock up to a panel or group knowing that they have had the corridor conversations with all the right people to smooth the path to getting the approvals. There is a balance between keeping this within good practice and not subverting the formal decision-making process. Especially if you believe that steering or key governance bodies come together to make collective decisions about issues, they had a chance to mull over independently beforehand. This approach may make for more efficient and faster decision making and how you do it that is key.

For a Sponsor, integrity is everything and should be the core of every choice you make. It's the first thing to ask yourself if you are not sure whether corridor conversations or backroom 'wheel greasing' is appropriate and indeed common decency. If it is expressly forbidden or you are asking people to make inappropriate compromises, using emotional blackmail or passive aggression, then it's a definite no.

Being self-aware and emotionally intelligent you recognise that good governance is a sensory process, not a hard-coded process. As long as you recognise the accountabilities of all concerned and that very rarely is everything black and white, then persuasion and insight using evidence and facts as well as guile to help others to conclude in their own minds is useful and powerful.

Decision makers in key governance bodies make assessments not just based on the data, but a depth of understanding of the issue, its context, the integrity, and the history of the presenter. Most executive decision-makers are combining the intelligence fed to them through project controls and other context information and submitted papers with their intuition.

If you need to build the understanding and confidence of a governance body member, you can do that without compromising ethics, rules, or integrity by using corridor conversations. It may be a less formal way for you to build rapport and credibility with them to smooth the upcoming governance decision. This may also be your opportunity to discuss any sensitive conflicts of interest or perverse commercial drivers that you have concerns about.

You may also know that panel members have different learning and decision-making styles and choose to address that outside of the formal process. For instance, some panel members seek the comfort of the detail of the engineering or the finance before making decisions. In busy project environments, a panel may not (and probably should not) have the time to have detailed discussions about technology solutions or forecasts within a governance meeting. It is completely appropriate to offer those decision-makers the opportunity to go over that detail with you in advance or to talk to the specialist in your team.

It's fine to be open about your purpose. You can say, "I'm bringing a big decision to the steering group next week and I want to find out if you have any major concerns that you need me to address in advance?". Asking key supporters or alliances of your projects to advocate for you is also an appropriate and often incredibly powerful strategy to smooth the governance wheels. These approaches, done well and respecting the accountability lines, are effective albeit 'unseen' Sponsorship, and not 'obscene' or subverting the process.

What not to do?

- Try to play panel members against each other.
- Mistake compromise for blackmail.
- Ask for favours that breach the rules (not to be confused with asking for appropriate derogations).
- Use corridor governance to push through poor decisions.
- Mislead panel members through inaccurate or inappropriate use of data – you will be found out!
- Disempower those with key accountabilities.

There is often additional complexity in the role of the Sponsor and that is that there is a named senior figure perhaps a director, executive, or even CEO who is called the Sponsor. Yet they are not the person likely to be doing the leg work of governance. They will not be writing change papers or rerunning business cases. Yet in a major project, their role is also vital in being the project's biggest ambassador in rallying the masses around the benefits of change. And yet we talk about single points of accountability being vested in a sponsor. There is a way to handle this well and that is to use the prefix such as an Executive Sponsor and a Delegated Sponsor or Sponsor's agent.

When deciding whether a project is in a fit state to proceed to the next stage Sponsors take vital decisions based on the information provided by the project team added to their knowledge. They do this because they must take into account factors beyond whether the technical solution can proceed. That is one element and Sponsors also consider human factors, funding, consents, land, reputation, stakeholders, risk appetite, and operational impacts and readiness.

Stage gates

Stage gates are a common part of project governance that Sponsors are involved with. Stage gates are undertaken at key decision points in projects. They normally have the recommendation to proceed or not to proceed often called a 'Go' or 'No Go' decision. They are often mandatory at key stages and some companies will also have optional stage gates which are held at the discretion of the Sponsor. The purpose of a Stage-Gate is to consider the level of risk in moving to the next stage of the project or making a key decision. The decision could be:

- Sign off on a design.
- Proceed to procurement.
- Proceed to award a contract.
- Proceed to the next project sage.
- Fund the next project stage.
- Approve a major change in the project.
- Drawdown risk funding.
- Close out the project.

The Stage Gate will be a combination of checking that paperwork is completed and compliant relevant to the project stage along with a review of project controls information and discussions with key individuals.

The Sponsor has the accountability to review all of the information and discussion and make a recommendation to proceed, proceed subject to conditions or pause and take corrective action or stop altogether.

Effective Sponsors take great care to lead Stage Gates well. They prepare in advance, create environments where difficult conversations can happen, and make decisions that are risk-based and relevant acknowledging that those aren't always the easiest or most popular decisions.

They know that the purpose of a Stage Gate is an honest assessment of risk, not sign-off and carry-on. They also know that pausing or attaching conditions means supporting the project team in the work that creates and managing the stakeholder messaging that will be required.

If you are using progressive assurance a Stage-Gate should be like a good annual appraisal. A chance to validate the ongoing progress updates and ratify any ongoing needs and goals. If you have little assurance or a hands-off approach to sponsorship then your Stage Gate may be like a badly managed annual approval. A store up of all the bad news that spills out in one emotionally charged session.

Sponsors have the choice of how they want Stage Gates to play out. Even if your organisation has not put in place robust and mature assurance you can choose to undertake some assurance activity of your own throughout the project. By explaining the purpose of this to the project team and working together on it everyone's life will be easier and your project's chances of success will be higher. You will also have far better Stage-Gate reviews.

Change control

In an ideal world Sponsors would commission projects with a fixed scope that delivers the benefits, agreed budget including risk allowances, suitable timelines, and resources. A project team would assemble, and it would be delivered, operationalised, and closed out. Change control would not be needed because even the things that went wrong would be accounted for within the risk allowance and duly drawn down. This has never happened on any project.

Change happens even to effective Sponsors and great project teams. It happens for a myriad of reasons. Some changes are predictable and containable within a risk allowance. An effective Sponsor will have delegated those and the accompanying risk allowance to the project manager. They will have put in place some checks and balances to be alerted if that risk allowance is being used faster than the risks are either materialising or being mitigated. They may also have a role in mitigating some of those risks and be involved with that.

Mostly though the Sponsor will leave the project manager and risk team to manage the changes that don't alter the overall cost, scope, benefits, timeline, or stakeholder expectations. So long as you have verified that they have a system of change control that manages this you can focus on other matters.

Those other matters may include the changes that a Sponsor has a role in. These are the major changes often driven by external factors. Concentrate your energies on strategic risks. Your role in managing the stakeholders and client if they do occur and how you will recover the position or move forward.

Your role is to minimise change control once your project is authorised. You will not be able to eliminate it so focusing on minimising it, being clear about its impact, and being realistic about what that means for the project is crucial. Changes at the strategic level have a habit of being:

- Unavoidable.
- Sudden and urgent change requests with long lead times to agree and finalise.
- Beyond your control or influence.
- High impact.

Many of these may be on your radar already if you are actively looking at the PESTLE risks to your project that we will look at in Chapter 9 Funding.

When these changes do occur, you must spend time properly assessing the impact with your project team. Make sure you have sufficiently understood and communicated the impact before the change is agreed upon. When the Client or Funder proposes a change, they should be made fully aware of the impact of the change and commit to it before the deliverer and supply chain are instructed of the change

The impact of change on all critical aspects of the project should be assessed.

The Sponsor needs to recognise that change during the construction of an infrastructure project comes at an exponential cost and might introduce significant risk to all aspects of the project. Any change should be managed through change control governance by the Sponsor in accordance with project and corporate governance.

Your project governance has to cover the governance of change control in a way that can assess, reject or approve it on time that gives certainty to clients and project teams of whether the change is going ahead and the agreed impacts. It must also formally consider and assess the impact on benefits and the likelihood of their successful delivery.

Top Tips for Successful Stage Gate Reviews

Anticipate

Expect that reviews will happen in advance of any investment decisions and Go/No-go choices. This is a core part of Sponsoring projects whether you are in the Public, Private, or Non-Profit Sector.

Plan

Successful Sponsors treat assurance activity as part of the day job. They use it as a way to measure how the project is performing and to forecast how it will perform in the future.

Research

Find out what methodology will be used and what level of review is needed. Consider what the areas of focus should be.

Prepare

You can never be overprepared for a Stage Gate. As Sponsors, you take a leadership role during these reviews. This is a growing area and one that you should learn how to navigate.

8
ASSURANCE

What is Assurance?

Project assurance and project governance are often talked about interchangeably. This happens especially with Sponsors because Sponsors have such a significant role to play in both.

Assurance can feed into good governance. There are important differences between the two and how they are undertaken and add value to projects.

Project assurance is a discipline that provides objective oversight of how the current performance of a project is predictive of future performance. Assurance also gives insight into how future performance can have an increased likelihood of success by making improvement recommendations.

Most companies will require a form of assurance to be carried out about their financial operations. Most people in corporate or government environments are familiar with assurance activity in the form of financial audits, audit committees, and external auditors assuring company accounts.

Project assurance is similar although has a much broader lens than the financial affairs of the project. It looks into a broader range of metrics and when done effectively the behaviours and leadership.

Why Assurance matters

Assurance on projects continues to grow and evolve. This growth area is one that Sponsors are expected to be able to navigate with ease. With a plethora of methodologies, approaches, frameworks, and levels of assurance it can be overwhelming.

Effective assurance takes into account behaviours, leadership, and culture. We recognise strong assurance as a predictor of success and risks rather than a process-oriented activity. A combination of report reviews, combined with interaction and interviews with stakeholders, site visits and observations will lead to far better assurance reports and recommendations.

What Sponsors need to know about it

As a Sponsor, you will want to know what is the assurance regime in your organisation. Are there mandatory assurance procedures and reviews that your project will have to go through? It is your accountability to understand these, know how they may impact the project, and what approvals may require an accompanying assurance report to get approval.

Assurance reviews can take different forms, more on that shortly. You can help prepare for these by making sure you have considered which will apply to your project and having the project team include that in the schedule and resource plan.

Types of Assurance

The most prevalent assurance regime is the lines of defence model.

In your organisation this could look like:

- 1st line of defence – project controls overseen by the Project Manager.
- 2nd line of defence – objective project assurance undertaken by the Sponsor.
- 3rd line of defence - objective project assurance commissioned by Sponsor/Board undertaken by assurance experts.

- External assurance – independent auditors or assurers.

The scale, structure, and maturity of your organisation will determine exactly how these lines of defence are determined. They are interrelated and hierarchal with the view that the first three lines feed information upwards and the assurance review is undertaken downwards.

In a mature organisation, Sponsors view assurance as playing a part in the success of projects. Assurance activities help identify areas that can be improved, verify what is working well, spot problems in advance, and offer helpful insights. Projects are pressured environments and often create teams who bond quickly and all pull together towards a common goal. There is no doubt that is a major success factor in projects. The counter to that is that sometimes groupthink occurs, and everyone is so focused on the plan for success and goal achievement that they miss something that could impede that success. Assurance is a methodology to step out of that group think and consider objectively against a framework for reviewing projects.

Great assurers are critical friends, they will help shine a light on what you might be missing giving you time to rectify or mitigate it. Using an assurance report to supplement your request for approvals at key governance stages is a powerful and mature way to turn assurance reviews into reassurance for your board, client, and stakeholders.

In less mature organisations assurance is sometimes viewed as being 'checked up on'. It can be seen as interference or unhelpful. The team and Sponsor are maybe resistant or absent giving the assurer a huge insight into where the challenges might lie!

A Sponsor leading a major project should be commissioning assurance to give them the knowledge they need to facilitate decisions or meet mandated assurance requirements. The trick to getting this right is creating a balance. Making sure that there is a sensible plan and that the team doesn't end up trapped in endless cycles of assurance at multiple levels that detract from their ability to deliver.

By building assurance in from the beginning this can be avoided. A culture of progressive assurance is one of the most effective approaches in modern project delivery. A great check and forecaster of success for Sponsors is to regularly ask:

- How are we doing?
- How did we reach that conclusion?
- How do we know that to be true?
- What does this tell us about our future?
- What needs to stop?
- What needs to start?
- What needs to continue?

In an overload of project details assurance can help take data, process it as information, and turn it into valuable knowledge.

Top Tips for Success Leading Assurance

Creative tension is part of assurance

Challenge by others is a good sense check on decision-making. It helps avoid groupthink, highlights risk and opportunity areas, and drives efficient problem-solving.

Intuition

Listen, see, and feel what your intuition is telling you. If you feel that you are not getting to the truth or the right answer, continue to ask questions, probe, and be curious.

Get comfortable

It can feel uncomfortable to ask others to challenge your ideas and perception or to find yourself having an uninvited challenge. Sponsors should be aware of that and help individuals understand that it is part of mature and successful cultures. It will drive positive outcomes, new solutions, and fresh ideas and brings to light that which was not known.

Be a leader

Sponsors should lead and behave in a way that creates the right environment and safe spaces for challenges.

There is gold in cognitive diversity

Take time and care to embrace diversity and value skills from different people and all levels of the project.

9

FUNDING AND COMMERCIAL RISK

What are Funding and Commercial risks?

In every project, someone is paying. In many projects, many people are paying!

A core part of the role of a Sponsor is making sure that there is adequate funding and/or financing in place at any given stage of a project. Sponsors also make sure that the correct permissions, contracts, and authorities are in place within their organisation to spend that funding. They should also advise the project team about any conditions or caveats that the funding came with to make sure these are met and discharged.

A key difference between the Sponsor and project manager here is that the project manager is often concerned only with the CAPEX. That is the Capital Expenditure for the Project.

That is the envelope that they have to deliver the project within including risk allowances.

The Sponsor has a wider view of the balance between CAPEX and OPEX. The OPEX is the Operational Expenditure for the business. As the person accountable for bridging the gap between project spend and ongoing business costs that may be impacted positively or negatively as a result of the project the Sponsor often has to take a helicopter view of changes to understand their impact on the other. If the project is running out of cash and the project team suggests cutting some scope that they don't see as an essential sponsor must understand what that will do to the future business OPEX before agreeing. Similarly, the CAPEX is being driven up by something that has almost no OPEX benefit or could easily be absorbed by the business without much OPEX impact. The Sponsor should assess this and bring it to a balanced answer that everyone who needs to, buys in to.

Why it matters?

So far we have covered several areas of a Sponsor's accountabilities in projects. Depending on where you work these will be relevant to a higher or lesser degree. Their significance to you will depend on something on your project, your organisation, and your style of sponsorship.

Every one of these has a strong commercial element. At every decision point, you will be making decisions using your commercial acuity. The world of the Sponsor is inherently commercial, and you make commercial decisions every day. Even when you don't realise it and even when others seek to absolve you of that responsibility. Remember when that happens (and it will happen) and you are tempted to hand over that responsibility, that you are likely to be the person who has to find more money if it runs out so why would you step away from that? Who seeks to benefit from you doing so? Not you, the organisation, or the project benefits.

As a Sponsor, if you want to be effective you cannot detach yourself from the commercial and funding aspects of your project.

The three commercial areas for Sponsors to pay particular attention to are:

- Funding and Finance
- Corporate Risk
- Commercial Acuity

Funding and finance

Private Sector

If you are sponsoring a project funded by a private company that you work for, you should have access to a significant amount of information. This along with your knowledge and experience of working there forms the basis of your internal stakeholder research.

If you are Sponsoring a project on behalf of a private company that you are not employed by you will be best advised to start doing some research. Look at key documents and see what they tell you about cash flow, debt ratios, profitability, and current risk exposures. Is it a publicly listed company (PLC)? If so you may want to set up an alert to follow their share price. Seek to understand what any changes to that share price mean about what is happening with that company. How does that correlate to any activity, project, or negotiation that you are involved in relating to your project?

Funding

Funding is the amount of money provided to pay for the project. This could be capital such as cash or borrowed money which is usually a form of finance.

Financing is money that is being loaned. This could be through a variety of mechanisms such as money borrowed from a bank or other financial institution, project financing provide by the delivery organisation, money leveraged against existing capital assets, or money raised through the sale of government-backed bonds.

If your project is being financed by a delivery organisation in a model such as private finance you should know this from the outset as it impacts how you structure any deals, write scope and plan, allocate and manage risk, and for operational hand back.

Each of these types of financing has different costs and implications for your project. As a Sponsor, you should be aware of where the funding and or financing is coming from and what that may mean for your project.

Therefore, your project funding may be financed through borrowing from one or multiple sources. They may have different conditions and or stipulations attached that you need to be aware of.

The cost of certain financing is subject to market and world economy volatility. This means that if your project is being funded by financing your costs may rise as a result of the cost of borrowing being higher. This is important to be aware of on any project where your project business case is marginal as the increased cost of borrowing money may mean that your business case is no longer viable.

Leading Corporate Risk

Risk management is part of the Role of a Sponsor.

You will need to build a working knowledge of:

- Risk.
- Opportunity.
- Corporate risk.
- Lessons Learned.
- Sponsors risk actions and landscape.

There is a big difference between what you need to know and understand about project risk and what you need to do about project risk. This relies on a fundamental basic: knowing the difference between the Sponsor and Project Manager's role in risk management.

As discussed in Chapter 7 best practice is for you to have set a risk allowance alongside the appropriate checks, balances, and governance. The project manager should be managing that using the agreed methodology such as active risk management or value management.

As a Sponsor, you remain focused on corporate and strategic risk. Making sure that you understand the corporate risk appetite and tolerances and keeping the project aligned with those is a critical success factor in any project. You should also be aware when these appetites change as the trickle-down will impact your project unless you can anticipate, manage or mitigate it.

Recognising and assessing how change may impact a project in terms of cost, schedule, quality, benefits, and stakeholder impacts is a key Sponsor activity and skillset throughout the project lifecycle. Scanning the horizon for what may be coming and thinking about how you could respond helps you avoid having to react.

New Sponsors often struggle with identifying the difference between the risk apportionment between them and the project manager. The delivery and construction risks get mixed up with the corporate risks and it leads to people tripping over each other on some risks, and no one focused on other risks. Corporate risks are often low-likelihood but high-impact risks that are filled with ambiguity. Those are the ones Sponsors need to focus on.

An excellent yet simple tool for Sponsors to use for this is PESTLE. PESTLE risks are mostly caused by external forces. It stands for:

- Political
- Economic
- Social
- Technological
- Legal
- Environmental

These are the risks unlikely to be in a project risk register but they may be in an Enterprise Risk Register (sometimes known as a bow tie risk register).

Examples of each of these types of risk are:

- Political – change of government.

- Economic – raised cost of borrowing.
- Social – Population increase.
- Technological – novel technology creates obsolescence.
- Legal – change in the law.
- Environmental – new carbon targets.

These risks occur at an enterprise or corporate level but may impact on individual projects. However, if every project were to model a risk allowance for each of them, we could never afford to deliver any projects again as the risk allowances would be so high. Instead, these risks have to sit either at the portfolio or organisation level. They may or may not have modelled or funded risk funds attached to them. Either way, if they look likely to occur the Sponsor has to consider how they might impact their project and what action and or funding may be required as a result. Update your PESTLE risk overview every six months at a minimum as a Sponsor.

There are also issues to consider. One method is to differentiate between risk and issues in this way

Risks:

- May or may not happen.
- Chance to mitigate or avoid it occurring.
- Maybe preventable.
- Potential solutions may be known.

- Can be scheduled, prioritised, assigned, and managed.
- Great risk management can give you time to think of all options and choose.
- Risk management is proactive.

Issues:

- Are happening.
- Have occurred or are occurring.
- May be irreversible.
- Are likely to be occupying much of your time.
- Get you into the press and boardroom.
- Cause stress and drive behaviours.
- Drives timelines for decisions.
- Issue management is reactive.

As sponsors, you will often be managing issues. It comes with the territory. You have a question to ask yourself though. Do you want to be a dream sponsor or a superhero sponsor? Superhero Sponsors are dreaded as they bring the crisis to any calm by wading into the risk that others are already managing, escalating before thinking and reacting instead of responding.

Commercial acumen

Commercial acumen is a Sponsor's understanding of economics, project, and organisational spending, contracting, and commercial policies, procedures, processes, systems, and governance.

Sponsors should learn how to:

- Read a balance sheet.
- Interpret the company accounts.
- Understand your market.
- Know what matters to who funds you (public sector this = government and customers and taxpayers).
- Difference between finance and funding.
- Know what impacts costs, prices, and value in your world.
- Choose tools to deal with commercial scale (probably not a calculator for projects).

Supply chains

How your supply chain performs and behaves commercially is a critical success factor for your projects. You may have a procurement or commercial team who leads activity here. A Sponsor should be aware of how the supply chain maturity and performance can influence success. How are your suppliers managing their supply chains? Do their suppliers lurch from one profit warning to another? Do they have a feast-and-famine approach to either awarding work or paying for contracted work? If they have gained a reputation for withholding payment to suppliers until the last second you should seek to understand the reasons behind that.

Is it because they are experiencing cash flow problems themselves? Are they immature organisations that don't understand that volatility in your supply chain can suppress commercial competition and add to risk and financing costs? Do they see themselves as hardball, tough commercial operators yet mistake commerciality and firmness with pedantry and outdated styles of management?

Are you keeping your entire supply chain cash-starved? If you are, be aware that this creates uncertainty and instability and will be influencing the pricing and risk allowances.

Are you offering incentives and ways for your supply chain to make ideas for improvements, value engineering, new approaches, or innovation?

Top Tips for Success

Take time to understand the commercial environment. Ask for advice and insights from others. This will help you understand cost control from the business, project, and commercial perspectives.

Where you can see commercial problems in projects that are being driven by policy procedure or culture within the origin, use your influence to suggest improvements to contracting and commercial arrangements at a strategic level.

Stay focused on corporate risks and issues whilst being aware of what is happening with project risks and assuring that they are being actively managed.

10

LEADERSHIP

What is Leadership?

Sponsoring projects is about leadership more than any other skill. Leadership is one of those skills that are described as soft skills, unlike hard skills which are technical. Of course, the irony is that soft skills are of course the hardest to define and teach yet have the most impact on the individual and the people they interact with on projects.

It is important to use your personal strengths and qualities and be an authentic leader of the project as a Sponsor. Focus on building strengths and being aware enough of any weaknesses you may have to prevent them from holding you back or damaging your project.

Why it matters

The role of a Sponsor means that you are the face of the project. Think of yourself as the personal advocate for the benefits that the project will bring.

Managing stakeholders is a lot more than sharing the good news with project supporters. It is about influencing and leading groups of people toward the goal of delivering benefits. Much of the time you may be gathering support, getting an agreement, or managing the disruption caused by people who do not support that goal or the impact of the project.

Despite the frameworks in this book and any training to help you understand how to Sponsor projects, there is no exact formula to make this easy. It is as complex as people are. Often that is both the beauty and the pain of being a Sponsor! It certainly means it is never dull because when you add human behaviour into complex projects and change anything can happen. Expecting the unexpected and being prepared to respond instead of reacting is what projects and clients need from an effective Sponsor.

Projects can be political and Political. Politics with the big P is about the decision-making and funding that comes from elected governments running a country. Small p politics are about human behaviour and power struggles in the workplace. If you abhor politics, you will find Sponsorship a challenge. If you can make peace with the fact that politics are a fact of life in every organisation and get clear on your role within that your life will be much easier. As a Sponsor, your role is to understand the politics, navigate and manage the politics and the Politics without falling into the trap of playing politics.

An analogy we use in training Sponsors is based in the French Alps. Mont Blanc in Chamonix is the highest Mountain in Western Europe. There are two ways down. One is via the Valle Blanche, which is 20 km of off-piste steep descent, only for experienced skiers. You must use a mountain guide, carry a lot of equipment, and be prepared for an arduous journey across crevasses and at risk of avalanches. Some years twenty people don't survive the descent across the Vallee Blanche.

Or you can take the Aiguille de Midi cable car down across some of Europe's most spectacular scenery to land safely in the gift shop.

Think of the dream Sponsor as one who can look at a project, recognise the challenges and complexity that will be an inevitable part of project delivery and benefits realisation, and choose to bring everyone down on the cable car safely and smoothly.

Projects are tough enough for whichever industry you are in, so the role of the Sponsor is to make that easier not harder. Leave the additional adrenaline for your leisure time.

Project teams have one of two views on Sponsors. We have categorised these as the dream Sponsor and the dreaded

Sponsor. Sponsors are human and no doubt you will have at some point strayed into dreaded Sponsor territory. To err is human and the best we can do is focus on doing our best as much of the time as we can.

The next section gives you a checklist of what the dream Sponsor and the dreaded Sponsor might do. It is a good exercise to check in with yourself on this regularly.

How do you know if you are a Dream Sponsor?

Be honest and ask yourself if you:

- Set and communicate strategic direction, vision, and benefits at the outset.
- Create strong relationships with your stakeholders and project team members.
- Use your influence and relationships to help the project.
- Are a visible advocate for the project and promote the benefits.
- Set the requirements and scope early on and explain the impacts of future change.
- Advocate for the project with challenging stakeholders or when there is difficult news.
- Know the warning signs that something is going wrong and act upon them.
- Act as a coach, mentor, decision-maker, or critical friend at appropriate times.

- Shield the project team from politics, change, and distractions.
- Constantly monitor the environment and give strategic direction.
- Set and communicate strategic direction, outcomes, vision, and goals for the project at the outset.
- Build strong relationships and leads on stakeholder issues.
- Know the warning signs that something is wrong and act before a crisis or problem arises.
- Know when to coach, when to mentor, and when to make a decision.
- Manage your influence and relationships to help the project.
- Invests time to build and maintain strong relationships with the Client, all functions, and the project management team.
- Are inquisitive, challenging, sensitive, and supportive.
- Clarify roles and responsibilities early on.
- Shield the project team from any unhelpful politics, change, and distractions.
- Explain the political and stakeholder environment in a way that informs schedule and risk management.
- Act as a visible ambassador for the project and helps to motivate the team.
- Constantly monitor the environment and gives strategic direction.

- Oversee a programme of progressive assurance.
- Use influence to build positive relationships that help the project.
- Focus on building team performance.
- Share bad news early and openly.

How do you know if you are a Dreaded Sponsor?

Do you ever:

- Demonstrate a lack of realism?
- Disregard advice from specialists or technical experts?
- Push too much risk into the future or the supply chain?
- Show a lack of ownership, direction, and leadership?
- Create over-complicated governance and structures?
- Fail to delegate?
- Escalate issues without attempts at compromise?
- Get caught up in playing politics instead of managing politics?
- Have a vague picture of the desired end state?
- Put massive expectations on the business or project team?
- Procrastinate instead of making decisions, delegating, or solving problems?
- Blame the programme team, the business, or the Client for project challenges?

- Focuses on the bureaucratic process at the expense of progress?
- Avoid difficult discussions until it is too late?
- Tries to project manage or engineer solutions instead of bringing disciplines together to solve issues?

What leadership qualities do you need to be a Sponsor?

Integrity is the most critical quality and strength of a sponsor. That applies at a personal and company level.

Qualities that great Sponsors are recognised for having are:

- Integrity.
- Ethical behaviours.
- Self-awareness.
- Empathy.
- Charisma.
- Honesty.
- Open-mindedness.
- Resilience.
- Leadership.
- Trust.
- Tenacity.
- Confidence.
- Empowering.
- Collaboration.
- Good Communication.

What experience do you need to be a Sponsor?

You should have a good understanding of:

- Projects, programmes, or portfolios – appropriate to which one you are working on.
- Project management methodology.
- Change management theory.
- Commercial acumen.

Giving Strategic Direction as a Leader

Part of your ongoing role is giving direction, motivation, and support throughout the project lifecycle to the project team. Sponsors understand that successful outcomes depend on everyone in the team sharing a common goal. Sponsors understand the competing demands of a business trying to cope with a change caused by a project. They also understand the political, financial, and demographic contexts.

Your communication style here is important. How do you talk to team members and internal and external stakeholders? Do you treat people as individuals and consider their perspectives? It is important to be able to translate any jargon into meaningful dialogue when speaking to those outside of the project and your organisation. You should understand relevant jargon and be able to navigate documents and situations where it is essential. Always avoid using jargon to isolate, impress or win negotiations.

Similarly, industry partners will anticipate that you have a reasonable understanding of their context, constraints, and objectives. If you don't then reach out to your peers and team for help.

Personal Effectiveness

Great Sponsors have high-performing levels of personal effectiveness. They are highly emotionally intelligent and regularly reflect on their behaviour and actions. They are self-aware and use tools to understand themselves and their behaviours.

They act with honesty and integrity to inspire confidence. They have the courage to act ethically and honestly even when that is very uncomfortable and puts them outside the group.

They keep commitments and avoid making commitments that they know they, the project, or organisation cannot meet. They follow up on commitments made or advise why it has not been possible to do so without attributing blame.

Effective Sponsors are highly reflective and consider their impact on others. They reflect on how that impact is in their normal state and under pressure. What are your tendencies under pressure, do you resort to task or people focus? What are the relative merits of either and when may they be problematic? What solutions might you apply to rectify any issues?

Take care to avoid behaviours that are aggressive, passive, or passive-aggressive when under pressure. Assertive behaviour is the required behaviour from Sponsors at all times.

Sponsors should plan how to stay engaged and monitor their own and others' engagement levels recognising the impact on performance. Then they take action to rectify dropping engagement levels or understand the causes.

Policy, process, and procedure do not have to stifle Sponsors' creativity. The role is most enjoyable when it as the role is one of ingenuity, innovation, and creative solutions. Compliance with process and policy should not be undertaken blindly or without challenge when it is leading to sub-optimal outcomes.

When Sponsors combine high levels of intuition with information to understand situations and solve problems, they generate alternative solutions. Cognitive diversity is a key factor in successful problem-solving. Sponsors can encourage wide participation by listening, encouraging, and keeping an open mind to other ideas.

Being open and transparent works beyond the project team. This includes being clear with external stakeholders about what information cannot be shared because it is unknown, or it is confidential. Build trust by being clear about when you simply cannot share what you know, when you genuinely don't have the information, or the answer is not yet known.

Can you articulate messages clearly to multiple groups? You will often have to be a two-way technical translator. You will need to translate the wishes of clients, stakeholders, and other business units into requirements. Can you translate technical language into plain English and use examples to help external or non-technical people understand?

Being highly collaborative and understanding the win-win nature of collaboration will reap rewards. Great collaboration relies on an ability to interface with others who have different learning, behavioural, and engagement styles authentically.

Sponsors regularly deal with ambiguity. Working in the white space means often finding gaps. Rather than thinking, "Not my job?" think, "Who's job is it, how will I make sure this is done?" The analogy that Sponsors conduct the orchestra rather than playing the first fiddle is a relevant one in that context.

Sponsors resolve the strategic issues and give the project clear direction on how to proceed. They understand the limitations of their own authority and can escalate without alienating stakeholders.

The busy Sponsor

Sponsors rarely have enough time to do everything that they would like to. They are among life's busy people. We live in an age of busyness. We have never been busier nor so desperate to stay busy and to communicate our busyness. There are multiple ways to stay busy. The availability and increasingly low cost of mobile technology bring huge benefits. We have access to our work and social network at our fingertips in almost any location. We have instant access to vast amounts of information. We can maintain relationships that would have floundered had they been dependent on landlines and letter writing.

But be under no allusion. It comes at price. The cost of being busy can be measured in two ways. Firstly, there is the cost to organisations. Costs can be direct as a result of people being busy rather than productive, more of which later. The costs can also be indirect though such as increased workplace absence from burnt-out employees, and decreased retention rates. As we learn more about fatigue and its impact on cognitive function, we realise that it could be errors made by frazzled staff or executives making important choices in projects whilst working upwards of sixty hours a week.

The second but not lesser cost is the cost to you. The stress of never feeling finished, frenzied races to deadlines, missed opportunities with friends and family, health issues, exhaustion, increased errors, less creative thinking the list goes on.

We can no longer pretend to not realise the impact of too much stress in the projects on our Sponsors (and others).

Does busy = productive though? Like all good answers, it depends. A never-ending cycle of "too busy" is stressful enough. Disconnect it from productivity and plug it into a project environment and you have a ticking time bomb.

Many busy Sponsors are productive. They are busy getting things done. The bustle around them is part of their persona and creates an energy around them that people want to engage with. It is a key part of their ability to get things done. They have it in balance and know when to stop being busy and rest, play, or relax.

What about the people who are always busy but never productive? They tend to make terrible Sponsors as their activity delays the project and they rarely enjoy the pace of the work.

Highly bureaucratic or less mature organisations can be especially adept at fostering this. If you wish to emulate this style, there are some key features that you will want to build in.

These include:

- All decisions made by the committee.
- Endless committee structures.
- Overly complicated governance structures (bonus if this help avoid any individuals making decisions).
- Meetings, meetings, meetings.

- Pre-meetings.
- Pre-pre-meetings.
- Multiple reviews of simple briefing notes authored and reviewed by multiple parties.
- Email as a main form of communication.
- Information is only being shared at meetings making knowledge dependent on attendance.
- Multiple project reports created with the same information drawn on different dates and discussed endlessly.

All of these are surefire ways to put busyness as an obstacle in the path to productivity. Let's be honest we will never eliminate meetings or emails. What we can do is take control of how we manage them.

As Sponsors, we can take some time off the hamster wheel to plan how to move from busy to productive. Then we can role model that for others to show that is what is valued on our projects. Productivity over activity every time. The good news is that productivity spreads faster than busyness as the majority of people come to work intent on doing a good job. Success is a huge motivator for people. The only successful projects are those that focus on productivity over busyness and busy boasting.

Except for the people busy being busy, we all want to be more productive in our work life. It makes us feel more successful, and more engaged and leaves more time and energy for our lives outside of work. Our understanding of work-life balance and how the success of one has a positive impact on the other has never been better understood or acknowledged so perhaps it is time to get less busy in our projects.

Playing the fiddle or conducting the orchestra

When you are in a role with the responsibility to manage people there is an implied command structure. It is a traditional part of the workforce culture. Employees will attend a workplace, managers will ask employees to carry out tasks. In the main, the employees will carry out the tasks and regularly be rewarded with a cash payment into their bank account in return for the task execution.

A fairly simplified management theory overlooks the complexities of how to achieve this. Not to mention a beleaguered profession of Human Resources people labouring under the weight of supporting managers in what is politely termed 'managing poor performance'. But in a nutshell, employees come to the workplace expecting to exchange labour for cash and to execute the wishes of a manager.

If we accept that as a fundamental truth, then anyone who has the role of manager can use this implicit command structure to get people to do things. This is rarely the role of the Sponsor. The Sponsor may also manage a team however their success as a Sponsor relies on their ability to influence a wide range of people, most of whom are outside their line management structure.

The single most effective way to do this is to always have in mind:

- What is the best outcome for the project.
- What is the best outcome for the business.

Keeping these in mind at all times is crucial. The role of the project team is to think of and deliver what is best for the project. It is their laser focus. The role of the sponsor is to keep that aligned with what the business also needs. As the link between the temporary unit, (the project) and the permanent unit, (the business) your role is to understand what both need when they are misaligned and bring them back into alignment.

Influencing people as a Sponsor is fundamentally different from the role as a manager and you have to think of them and develop yourself taking into account these differences. Start by looking at yourself as a leader. There are resources such as Insights and Myers Briggs that will help you look at your key strengths. 360 reviews will give you the insight of others to alert you to any blind spots you may have. Whilst it is best to focus on playing to your strengths and developing these you will also benefit from understanding the impact of any weaknesses or blind spots on your ability to influence others.

One of the most powerful questions we can ask ourselves as Sponsors is:

- What kind of leader do I want to be?

If the answer isn't immediately obvious consider the people you have admired, consider asking for mentoring or just hang around with those people and watch and learn from them.

Understanding yourself and being congruent with your values has far more integrity than stretching into something you are not. This isn't at odds with being a chameleon, as mentioned in Chapter 2 on Stakeholder management. Being a chameleon is not about being false or putting on a personality. It is about adapting your personality and range of ability to interact with people in a way that is still true to who you are.

Doing versus making sure it is done

The approach that a Sponsor should take in projects is well described as being the difference between 'Playing the Fiddle and Conducting the Orchestra'

The role of the Sponsor will only lead to fatigued Sponsors if the Sponsor starts to pick up any unactioned items or try to prop up the project. A more successful approach is to have a combination of skills at play and processes in use to make sure that work is done rather than always being the doer.

Consider the following:

How are you monitoring progress? Do you read project reports and assume they tell you all you need to know? Do visit the site or the place where the change is being implemented? If not, how do you harness your instincts to combine what they tell you with the data and reports being presented to you? What information is assuring you that you can provide the Client and stakeholders with reassurance that all is well?

Where there is no one undertaking an activity can your secure additional resources or support instead of picking up the work? That is the difference between strategic and tactical responses.

Resilience

Sponsors are the ambassador for the project and are seen as the face of the project. At times you will inevitably face some adversity because of that. It may be in various forms and for various reasons. These could include:

- Project delay.
- Cost overrun.
- Lack of integration.
- Project accidents/incidents.
- Negative publicity due to your project or organisations.

- Negative publicity due to links with a stakeholder or supplier.

Some of it may feel very personal and may be given in the context of personal comments. Sponsors have to develop a certain armour and anticipation of this. If you represent the project to many people that then means accepting the rough with the smooth. It would be trite to say simply ignore personal comments and switch off from your day job.

That is a strategy that you may be able to take and if it works for you with no adverse effects then all is well and good. However, if you are just burying the feelings then in the long term is not good for your mental health, self-esteem, or resilience as a Sponsor.

The ability to absorb or ignore criticism, respond appropriately, and cope well is worth working on if you want to stay effective, Unfortunately, the only guide to avoiding ever having to deal with project adversity is to avoid working on projects.

Instead, some tips to deal with it are:

- Don't absorb it personally even if it is launched at you.
- Seek good counsel.
- Talk to a trusted colleague or friend.
- Listen to hear what the person or people are angry about.

- Find what replenishes you - fresh air, exercise, travel, nature, walking, talking music, and do it as often as you possibly can.
- Build a network of other Sponsors you can talk to.

Keeping your resilience up is as critical in the good times and the bad.

Top Tips to Go from Busy to Productive

Emails

- Use automatic rules to file emails that don't need read immediately in folders for reading at your convenience. It's easy to do on Outlook.
- Have all emails that you are 'cc'd' into go to a separate 'cc' folder. This allows you to focus on emails that are directed to you.
- You can even progress to the 'auto delete' of emails if you dare!
- There is also the old-fashioned and perhaps radical option of having a conversation instead of sending or replying to an email. As well as reducing your inbox you get the benefits of social interaction.

Meetings

- Check why you are being asked to attend. Most people are nice. They may add people to avoid you feeling excluded or because of hierarchical considerations. If you don't need to be there don't go but do tell people that you are not attending.
- No agenda = no attendance. Productive people don't have time to turn up and see if there is anything to have a meeting about.
- Embrace cancelling meetings when there is no notable change or update. Maybe also consider re-setting your meeting frequency. Perhaps frequent meetings were required initially and now they aren't. You can always increase again in the future if things change.
- Avoid trying to defy the laws of physics. Also known as the back-to-back meeting day, sometimes with a few locations built in. Until teleportation is on offer this is a guaranteed busy maker and stress builder in employees. I'm thinking of starting a movement to campaign for the 50-minute meeting invite.

Personal Effectiveness

- Find out your best time for working and try to build time in your day for your most challenging/creative/detailed work to be done then. Match how you

work best to when you work best, and you are guaranteed to be productive.
- Challenge your daily or weekly routine to see if what you are doing is keeping you busy or making you productive.
- Prioritise. You don't have to do everything. Like all great leadership theories, there is a 4-box model that can help. Start using this approach and before you realise it this will become your habit.

Do it now	Dump it now
Delegate it now	Diary it for the future

This is from Stephen Covey's book The Seven Habits of Highly Effective People which is a text we frequently recommend to Sponsors.

Tops tips on scheduling for Sponsors

Project heartbeat

Put your regular meetings and any key dates or milestones into your diary. Consider any key decisions, changes, or gate reviews. Does it look like there are any conflicts? Do you have enough lead time for the governance and assurance around those activities?

Clients

Take time to think about how your Client wants to be informed this year and plan for it. Not sure if they prefer face-to-face, lengthy reports, or a quick call? Ask them and then include that in your diary. One thing clients always want is to be the first to hear important project news.

Stakeholders

Is there anything happening this year that could impact a stakeholder's view of your project? Whether positive or negative make sure you know, diary the event or milestone and check in with them around this time. Is there a time they are really busy? Put that in the diary too and show that you respect their priorities.

Project managers

Even if you see the Project Manager regularly it can be easy to get caught up in day-to-day project issues. Schedule a regular time for both of you to sit down and talk. You need time to talk about any issues, general progress, and whether they need any help from you.

11

PROJECT LIFECYCLE

This chapter gives Sponsors guidance on what to expect and at times to do at a different stage in the project lifecycle. It cannot be exactly replicated each time because the nature of what the Sponsor deals with is the grey areas, the unexpected, the ambiguity, and the curveballs.

It is useful to think about how some of what a Sponsor may expect to deal with can be mapped against a lifecycle. This can give the Sponsor the chance to think not only about what they might expect to encounter but also to anticipate and plan for some eventualities. This in turn helps mitigate the risk of investment being made or used inappropriately at any stage in the lifecycle.

This is an example of what a process for sponsoring a project from initial concept to close out of the project could look like.

With experience, Sponsors can flex and adapt this approach to create their own or they can adapt it to the project lifecycle approach used by the project or organisation.

It is easier to be the guiding mind of the project throughout its lifecycle if you have a framework, to begin with.

Project lifecycle approaches

Project management has several different approaches to project lifecycles. There are various methods such as lean, waterfall, and agile. Some of these are best suited to certain industries or project types, Indeed one company may use more than one method. There are training courses that teach each of the types of methods and how to apply them at all stages.

For Sponsors, we use a lifecycle that can overlay into any of the methods. We at times find Sponsors adrift trying to figure out where the actions they need to take fit into traditional project management lifecycles.

Rather than try to replicate how each method translates to Sponsorship activity the following table shows the overview of our Effective Sponsorship Lifecycle which Sponsors can relate to their practice area.

There are 5 stages of the Effective Sponsorship Lifecycle. These are shown in the table below along with some examples of our suggested Sponsor role and priorities during each stage.

Stage	Initiation and authorisation.	Planning and Design.	Delivery and Monitoring.	Handover, embed change benefits delivery.	Closeout, Benefits secured & measured.
Sponsor role	Help establish idea at strategic level	Manage strategic alignment	Project advocacy	Facilitate handover	Confirm close out
Sponsor role	Identify high level requirements	Define requirements & scope Create options	Control scope & Limit change	Confirm Requirements delivered	Confirm benefits delivered
Sponsor role	Identify type of project team needed	Establish project team	Provide support to project team	Provide support to project team	Agree completion
Sponsor role	Identify stakeholders	Understand & Map stakeholders Build relationships	Stakeholder management	Stakeholder management	Close out Stake holders
Sponsor role	Start Governance processes	Initiate project governance	Lead governance processes	Lead governance processes	Lead completion close out governance
Sponsor role	Start Benefits & Business case	Update benefits & Business case	Track & manage benefits	Confirm Benefits delivery	Measure & confirm benefits delivery
Sponsor role	Gather cross business support & input	Plan future state	Prepare for handover	Strategic support for handover	Finalise issues
Sponsor role	Agree assurance plan	Establish assurance	Ongoing assurance	Into service assurance	Lead Lessons learned
Sponsor role	Initiate funding and approvals	Identify further approvals & funding	Problem solve strategic issues	Finalise funding & accounts	Close out funding

When Sponsors are using the Effective Sponsorship lifecycle they can assess what activity they should be undertaking based on the 5 key actions of an Effective Sponsor. Each key action has a subset of 20 activities that cover the most common ones that Sponsors must do.

A highlight of this is shown in the table below:

Key Action	Example activity
Lead	Lead the Business Case and track benefits realisation, gateway reviews, governance, and assurance processes.
Define	Define project objectives and outcomes.
Collaborate	Collaborate with all stakeholders including funders, project team, suppliers, operations, and steering group.
Represent	Represent the needs of all business functions and the Client in the project meetings, discussions, and decisions.
Act	Act as an ambassador for the change. Act to solve problems, make decisions, and role model the corporate values or objectives.

Using a combination of understanding where you are in the Effective Sponsorship Lifecycle and choosing from the 5 key actions of an Effective Sponsor is a tool for Sponsors to use whether unsure of what to do next or planning for the next stages.

When things feel uncertain you can use these two tools as a matrix. Look at the Effective Sponsorship Lifecycle and decide what stage your project is in. Think about what role you play as a Sponsor at that stage and what be coming in the next stage.

Next, look at the 5 key actions of an Effective Sponsor and decide which one or ones you need to do now and which you are most likely to need to do next.

Using these tools will help you apply a consistent way to think about your role and what you need to d and anticipate to reduce some of the surprises that sometimes are an adventure that we can lean into but sometimes come so frequently they almost bowl us over.

Projects will never be fully predictable. If we are honest with ourselves we do not work as project Sponsors because we love predictability. We do it because we love the chance to solve problems creatively, work on legacy projects, and do interesting work that we care about. We love supporting a difficult and worthwhile project from inception to benefits delivery. We enjoy using our people skills and network to garner support for the idea and harness that into advocacy for our project, solving strategic challenges as we go.

We want to work in a way that brings the project team and the business through a period of healthy tension, and challenges and into a smooth operation with a sense of pride that all can share in.

Closing a book is like a Sponsor closing a project. It is a time to celebrate a project you have enjoyed being part of it, joy at completion, and sadness that it is over. It is that time here and there is no avoiding it.

I hope that this book has helped clear up some of the mystery that surrounds Sponsorship. I hope it has given you clarity and tools you will continue to use to hone your skills and make your work life more effective.

You now know:

- What is the role of the Sponsor is.
- The key aspects of the role.
- Some tools to use.
- Tips to help.
- How to be personally and professionally effective.
- Why your role is so crucial.

You now:

- Can apply these skills and tools.
- Can continue to develop yourself by honing your skills.
- Have the information to help with being more effective and enjoying your role.
- Have sufficient knowledge of the how and own the why.

Sponsorship is the most exciting and impactful role you can play in a project, and I wish you the best of success, adventure, and enjoyment throughout it.

Stay curious and embrace change with enthusiasm, it is why you are here.

ABOUT THE AUTHOR

Carol is a career Sponsor, an international expert in Sponsorship, and the founder and CEO of a global consulting firm, See Change International Consulting Ltd.

She founded the business to be able to provide the service that she often sought out and rarely found as a Sponsor. Carol has held senior executive roles as a Vice President and National Head of Sponsorship in organisations in the UK and internationally with accountability for investments and projects in the multi-billions.

As someone who has always embraced change, she enjoys helping others navigate through change and projects toward positive outcomes. Whether that be building mega projects, training Sponsors, or helping organisations embed and improve their Sponsorship capability, change is her comfort zone.

Carol loves working with Sponsors and projects as an international speaker, trainer, coach, and consultant.

She loves to meet people and travel and has lived in many cities, several countries, and a couple of continents....so far.

See Change International Consulting Ltd.

We are an international business specialising in all aspects of Project Sponsorship. We sponsor complex projects, programmes, and portfolios in various industries.

We help clients deliver benefits and successful projects by providing training, coaching, sponsorship, and consultancy. We help organisations embed and improve their Sponsorship capability and coach, train, and develop Sponsors at all stages of their careers.

We are seasoned practitioners and thought leaders in the Sponsorship profession.

We can also help you connect with the talent, skills, and resources you need across three continents.

See Change International promotes the values of public transport and ethical business behaviours including social, humanitarian, and sustainable environmental principles.

We've worked with some of the biggest organisations and corporate clients, and are proud to facilitate connections, projects, and partnerships that are creating sustainable, positive change in the world. We know that for your company, good business is about more than just projects, it's about leaving the world better than you found it. We feel the same way.

Competence Framework and Maturity

In the absence of a competence framework for Sponsors by any professional institutes See Change International has created a competence framework for Sponsors, a maturity map for organisations with Sponsors, and an Effective Sponsorship Lifecycle. We would be delighted to work with your organisation to introduce these tools.

You can find more information and useful resources on www.see-changes.com

You can sign up for our newsletter 'Sponsoring Effective Projects' on LinkedIn for regular advice, tips, and tools for sponsoring projects.

www.see-changes.com

linkedin.com/in/carol-deveney

ACKNOWLEDGMENTS

There are so many Sponsors for me to thank. I have worked with, met, messaged, or been in APM or other institutes with many of you. You've been amazingly supportive of my journey and this book. Sponsors are a special breed of people that I love to be around. To all of you who are always sharing your stories, offering support, and all whilst spinning those plates, thank you for all of it.

To all of my clients who put their investment of faith in me and my work. Know that I always find it a privilege and a pleasure to work with you.

Andy T thank you for all of your invaluable advice, support, and friendship. You were the first to tell me I was making the right decision and to share so much of your own journey with me.

Thank you to Alan and Susan who put their faith in me and inducted me into the world of Sponsorship. I never underestimated the privilege.

I have had many amazing opportunities since then. They were given to me by people who were willing to risk hiring someone who will always question the status quo, drive change relentlessly and try new ideas. To Kiernan, Neil, Jo and Phil thank you for the opportunities that allowed my entrepreneurial spirit and curiosity to flourish.

Thank you to Spencer Gibbens for the analogy of Playing the fiddle versus conducting the Orchestra, Helen Goulding, for the concept of Nightmare and Dream Sponsor, and Martin Samphire, for the concept of Executive and Delegated Sponsor.

Bill's insights as a client helped shape and inform not only this book but also how we train Sponsors across the world.

Thank you to those I interviewed as part of this book who couldn't be named and who shared their stories, insights, and advice. I hope I have done you justice.

Brian, thanks for coming along when I said I'm going to leave my job, go to the beach for three months, write a book, and start a business for Sponsors. Declan thank you for being part of that business, as you said the railway finally got you.

To my Dad who said ' I think you would like being a Sponsor' and my Mum who has always told me I can do anything, especially when the odds are against it, thank you for everything and I'm glad you were both right!

Chris, Karen, Eireann, Cavan and Niamh you are the ultimate cheerleaders and now that I have finished this book I know you will have your pom poms out to help me celebrate. I also now have the time to do it!

Sponsors are people gatherers at heart and I am no different. I have so many people around that me have enriched my life that the risk is too high in listing them I leave one out. Thank you to all of my friends and family, you know who you are.

I would like to thank Authors and Co for all of their help throughout. This is the first book I wrote and the second to be published with their support.

Abigail Horne's advice to change the publishing sequence has proved invaluable. Thank you, Abi. One day I'll explain why it made so much of a difference on a personal and professional level. All that matters is that you knew it and you advised me well.